The Zen Writings Series

The Hazy Moon of Enlightenment

THE
HAZY MOON
OF
ENLIGHTENMENT

On Zen Practice III

Hakuyu Taizan Maezumi and Bernard Tetsugen Glassman

Zen Writing Series

Center Publications, Los Angeles, California

Zen Writings Series

Series Editors: Hakuyu Taizan Maezumi, Bernard Tetsugen Glassman

On Zen Practice: Foundations of Practice (1976)
On Zen Practice II: Body, Breath and Mind (1977)
To Forget the Self: An Illustrated Guide to Zen Meditation (1978)
The Hazy Moon of Enlightenment: On Zen Practice III (1978)
The Way of Everyday Life (1978)

The Hazy Moon of Enlightenment, *published under the joint auspices of the Zen Center of Los Angeles and the Institute for Transcultural Studies, is one volume in the Zen Writings series, a monographic series comprising two new titles each year. Subscription rate for one year: $10.00 in the U.S. and Canada, $15.00 foreign. For two years: $18.00 in the U.S. and Canada, $28.00 foreign.*

For further information, contact: Center Publications, 905 S. Normandie Ave., Los Angeles, California, 90006. © *1977 by Zen Center of Los Angeles, Inc. Printed in the United States of America.*

Library of Congress Cataloging in Publication Data:

Maezumi, Hakuyu Taizan
The hazy moon of enlightenment

(The Zen Writings series)
Includes index.
1. Spiritual life (Zen Buddhism) 2. Enlightenment (Zen Buddhism)
I. Glassman, Bernard Tetsugen, joint author. II. Title. III. Series.
BQ9288.M33   294.5'444   77-81974
ISBN 0-916820-05-X

Though clear waters range to the vast blue autumn sky,
How can they compare with the hazy moon on a spring night!
Most people want to have pure clarity,
But sweep as you will, you cannot empty the mind.

—Keizan Zenji

CONTENTS

FOREWORD

It is a privilege to write this foreword, which seems to mark a joining of the clarity of Zen tradition with the vividness of Tibetan tradition. In the United States, Zen has been the vanguard of buddhadharma, and it remains genuine and powerful. Its simplicity and uncompromising style have caused Western minds to shed their complexities and confused ideology. It has been remarkable to see Western students of Zen giving up their territory of ego purely by sitting, which is the genuine style of Shakyamuni Buddha. On the other hand, some people tend to glamorize their ego by appreciating Zen as a coffeetable object, or by dabbling in Zen rhetoric. Another problem has been fascination with cultural beauty, causing a failure to appreciate the austerity of the true practicing tradition.

As we know, "Zen" derives from the Chinese word *ch'an*, from the Sanskrit *dhyana*, meaning "meditation." In Tibetan it is *samten*. *Sam* means "cognitive mind" and *ten* means "steady." So samten, or Zen, is the notion of being in a state of stillness. In the *Dasabhumika Sutra* and the *Samadhiraja Sutra*, the Buddha talks about the means for practicing dhyana as cultivating the right motive, which is refraining from fascination with external sensory input. This technique has become one of the most powerful in overcoming theism and psychological materialism. Theism in this case is belief in an external savior, which leads to a fundamental dualism between self and others.

Psychological materialism is shielding oneself from the fear of death and decay through intellectual and aesthetic pursuits, trying to make oneself into a perfect work of art.

The profounder right motive, according to the *Tathagatagarbha Sutra*, is to awaken oneself to buddha-nature. Whenever doubt arises, one should cut through it; doing this, one finds behind it a state of brilliant wakefulness. The doubt which must be cut through is not so much intellectual uncertainty, but general slothfulness.

There are the different traditions of sudden and gradual paths to realizing buddha-nature. But it seems that the conclusion is the same, no matter how suddenly it dawns. Still, every path has a beginning, middle and end. Therefore sudden could be called gradual, and vice versa. As long as there is a need for clearing away clouds of confusion, there is a path. In fact, the concepts of sudden and gradual are merely mental flickers. In either case, when the student begins to have a longing or passion for buddha-nature as his prize, that in itself is an obstacle. Sometimes we find that very dedicated students have difficulty in making progress. When there is some freeness combined with tremendous exertion and practice, then buddha-nature begins to shine through. But it seems to be dangerous to talk too much about buddha-nature: we might formulate a mental image of it.

When this twofold right motive of refraining and awakening begins to develop in the practitioner, then the sense of stillness begins to dawn. In this case, stillness is not something distinguished from motion; it is stillness without beginning or end. In this stillness, the five eyes of the Buddha begin to open, so that finally dhyana gives birth to prajna, which is the sixth paramita of the bodhisattva path. Prajna, or discriminating awareness, is a two-edged sword which cuts oneself and others simultaneously. At the level of the emergence of prajna, the experience of samadhi becomes apparent. Samadhi means "being there" or "holding acutely." According to the sutras, there are millions of samadhis, but they all simplify into two approaches: *sugata*, which is "well-gone," and *tathagata*, "gone as it is." Both achieve the *tathata*, which is "as it is."-

It is very soothing to talk about these things; however, if there is no exertion and wakefulness we are not even fingerpainting, but deceiving ourselves in the name of the dharma. I feel that the existence of the practice tradition is the only hope. It alone can wage war against ego. It alone is the way that we can comprehend the dharma.

The Venerable Taizan Maezumi Roshi's teaching has caused true

Zen to penetrate into people's minds and has cut through the trappings of their ego-oriented intentions. I have strong conviction that through his wisdom, buddhadharma will shine into the world, dispelling the darkness of samsaric confusion and bringing the gentle rain of compassion.

> Riding the horse of mirage
> Watching the sea of stars
> Blossoming great eastern sun.

Chögyam Trungpa
The Kalapa Camp
December, 1977

PREFACE

The three books in the "On Zen Practice" trilogy—*On Zen Practice: Foundations of Practice, On Zen Practice II: Body, Breath and Mind,* and *The Hazy Moon of Enlightenment*—reflect the teachings of Taizan Maezumi Roshi through three generations, and include talks by Roshi himself, by his teachers and by his students. The trilogy, therefore, presents Zen practice as it existed in Japan, as it has existed in the transitional phase in which a Japanese Zen master presents it to an American audience, and as it is manifesting itself in its new environment, with American students teaching it in the American idiom.

Dogen Zenji, the founder of Japanese Soto Zen, describes practice as a spiral of four phases. The first is *raising the bodhi-mind*, raising the desire for enlightenment; in other words, vowing to ourselves and to others that we will accomplish the Way, attain the realization of who we are, together with all sentient beings. The second phase is *practice*, putting our full effort into these vows and giving them life by striving toward the accomplishment of the unaccomplishable. The third is *realization*; with strong vows and determination to accomplish the Way, this steady, consistent practice ultimately results in realization, understanding, insight. And the fourth is *nirvana*, letting go of what we have realized and renewing our vows to again accomplish the Way, practice, realize and let go. This spiral continues endlessly, increasing in depth and in breadth, encompassing all things.

On Zen Practice: Foundations of Practice, the first book in the trilogy, explores the fundamental questions we ask when we first give rise to an aspiration to practice: What is practice? Why practice? What is effort? What is sesshin? *On Zen Practice II: Body, Breath and Mind*, goes on to describe aspects of Zen practice in detail and includes articles on koan practice and shikan-taza, breathing, gassho and bowing, and receiving the precepts.

The present volume, *The Hazy Moon of Enlightenment*, presents the third and fourth phases of this endless spiral. Parts one and two, "Enlightenment" and "Delusion", tell what there is to realize—what enlightenment means, what delusion means, and why Dogen Zenji says that enlightenment is delusion. The last part, "Enlightenment in Action," presents the active state of nirvana, the state of letting go and going on, as embodied in the eight awarenesses of the enlightened person. Both the book and the trilogy end at this point, but as Dogen Zenji says, our practice is endless. In reality, the end of this book brings us back to the first volume, *On Zen Practice*, in which we again renew our vows and ask, Why practice? Who am I?

Another way of looking at our practice is revealed by examining the following koan: "Master Shih-hsuang said, 'How will you step from the top of a hundred-foot pole?'" Since we are always on top of a hundred-foot pole, the question asked here is, "Being where you are right now, how do you go one step further? What is at the end of that one step?" Taking that step, we realize what we are, what life is, but we again find ourselves on top of a hundred-foot pole, clinging desperately to the tip, not wanting to fall off and yet knowing we must go further. So again and again we have to take that step and find out what's at the end of it. On top of the high mountain, we can see boundless mountains above. Reaching to the highest of them, still we can see boundless clouds heaped one on top of another, and beyond that the vast and empty sky endlessly expanding. Let's take those steps together and accomplish the Way with all beings.

Grateful student of Taizan Maezumi Roshi,
Tetsugen Glassman

EDITOR'S NOTE

All discussions and Dharma dialogues in *The Hazy Moon of Enlightenment* were led by Bernard Tetsugen Glassman, Sensei. All other chapters but two were originally teisho (formal Dharma talks) given by Taizan Maezumi Roshi and edited for inclusion in this book. Chapter Two, "Approaches to Enlightenment," was written by Daiun Harada Roshi; Chapter Five, "Sitting Down in the World of Enlightenment," was written by his Dharma successor and Maezumi Roshi's teacher, Hakuun Yasutani Roshi.

Chinese names are given in the original Chinese pronunciation according to the standard Wade-Giles system of romanization even when they may be better known to readers in Japanese. However, the Japanese name has been added in parentheses when the name first appears, and occasionally in other contexts to avoid confusion. The reader may also consult the Chinese-Japanese name glossary at the back of the book.

Chinese and Japanese words are set in italics when they first appear and in Roman thereafter, except when, in the judgment of the editors, they have become standard American Zen parlance, in which case they are not italicized at all.

Finally, the asterisk (*) has been used, as sparingly as possible, to refer the reader to the glossary when an unfamiliar word appears whose meaning is essential to the understanding of a passage. Since so many of the terms used in this book may seem unfamiliar to the average reader, we encourage the reader to refer often to the extensive glossary provided at the back of the book. It was intended to be consulted frequently as a supplement to the text.

Part One
Enlightenment

ONE

The Sound of Enlightenment

Taizan Maezumi Roshi

There is a famous haiku by the Japanese poet, Matsuo Basho (1644–1694):

> Old pond
> Frog jumps in
> The sound of water

Not only was Basho a master of haiku, he also studied Zen under a priest by the name of Buccho, with whom he had a close friendship in addition to their teacher-student relationship. When he composed this famous haiku, he was living in Tokyo in a small hut. One day, after a brief rain, Buccho Zenji visited Basho, and as a greeting asked: "How's your understanding these days?" Basho responded, "Rain has passed; green moss moistened." Buccho Zenji probed further, "Say something more." At that instant, Basho heard the plop of a frog jumping into a pond, so he answered, "Frog jumps in/The sound of water." The poem consists of seven and five syllables; being a poet, Basho naturally expressed it in a very rhythmic way. And Buccho Zenji approved his realization. Later Basho told his senior students, "I want you to add a phrase of five syllables to the beginning of this." Somehow Basho didn't like any of the lines they came up with and added this first line himself: "Old pond."

Zen master Sengai, (1750–1837) whose paintings have become famous in this country in recent years through the work of Dr. D. T. Suzuki, painted a picture of a frog and accompanied it with the following poem:

> Old pond
> Basho jumps in
> The sound of water.

Another time he drew a picture of a frog and wrote:

> Old pond
> Frog jumps in
> The sound.

"Of water" was eliminated. Another poet by the name of Shiken Taguchi saw that picture and complained, "This is not a haiku." Sengai replied, "Yes, I know. I want you to hear what kind of sound it is."

Isn't that a nice story? What kind of sound is it?

In the first poem, Sengai says that Basho jumps in. It's easy to see that Sengai sees no division between Basho, himself and the sound of water made by the frog jumping in. In other words, the subject-object relationship has disappeared. Then Sengai says further, "Frog jumps in/The sound." Here Sengai is not expressing the sound of something else, but he is manifesting himself as the sound of everything, the form of everything, the color of everything.

Buddhism is the teaching of awakening, the way of enlightenment. And enlightenment is the realization of the unity and harmony of ourselves and externals. It is the way of awakening from a bad dream, in which we divide ourselves from everything else, everybody else, creating all kinds of problems and difficulties. In short, enlightenment is realizing this sound, the sound of oneself, the sound of one's true nature.

Twenty-five hundred years ago, when Buddha saw the morning star after six years of meditation on the true meaning, the true face, the true nature of life, what did he realize? In the first chapter of the *Denkoroku* (The Transmission of the Light), Keizan Zenji writes: "Shakyamuni Buddha, seeing the morning star and attaining the

Way, exclaimed, 'I and the great earth and all beings have simultaneously accomplished the Way.'" What does that mean? We can say that Basho saw this morning star when he heard the sound of the water. In the same manner, Shakyamuni Buddha saw or heard the sound, whatever it was caused by. Our practice is to hear this sound, to see this form. We can express it sophisticatedly: this "soundless sound," this "formless form." This formless form is not something transparent that we can't see, but rather the opposite. The very form of all of us and of everything in the universe is nothing but this formless form.

In the *Avatamsaka Sutra* it is said that one is all, all is one. And in the *Lotus Sutra* (*Saddharma Pundarika*) it says, "All dharmas are reality (real form) itself." To see this is the moment of enlightenment.

Regarding the *Lotus Sutra*, I still recall quite vividly that when I was studying under Watanabe Genshu Zenji, the Chief Abbot of Sojiji, he told me that the very spirit, the very essence expressed in the *Lotus Sutra* is "Penetrate deep into samadhi and see the Buddhas in the ten directions." And Dogen Zenji says, "To clarify life and death is of vital importance." In the *Lotus Sutra* this grave importance is explained as "opening the eye of Buddha's wisdom." Zen Master Shih-t'ou Hsi-ch'ien (Sekito Kisen), Dharma grandson of the Sixth Patriarch, also clearly states, "the important matter is to awaken Buddha's wisdom."

Sometimes we hear it said that we shouldn't seek after enlightenment as such. "We shouldn't seek after" is okay. What this really means is that we shouldn't seek after something outside ourselves. We've got to "seek after," we've got to seek after ourselves, who we really are. That's what all the patriarchs and masters did. Without seeking and searching, we won't get anywhere. So please, let's take the time to patiently, diligently go on to clarify this grave, important matter.

As to the nature or characteristics of the practice of the Soto and Rinzai schools, we can say that the Rinzai school tends to emphasize the importance of attaining and clarifying enlightenment, while in the Soto school, although of course it is important, we rather emphasize the importance of practice itself. This doesn't mean that we don't need to acquire the Buddha's wisdom; it's still essential, but definitely we should go far beyond that. That's what Dogen Zenji means in the *Fukanzazengi* (Universal Promotion of the Principles of

Zazen) when he says: "Suppose one gains pride of understanding and inflates one's own enlightenment, glimpsing the wisdom that runs through all things, attaining the Way and clarifying the mind, raising an aspiration to escalade the very sky. One is making the initial, partial excursions about the frontiers, but is still somewhat deficient in the vital way of total emancipation."[1] He is not putting down enlightenment, he is just mentioning that it is not the final state. In his time, the general tendency was that, once having attained that state, people didn't practice any longer, or even said that they could do whatever they wanted to do. His statement warns against such a tendency. There is no end to how much we can accomplish.

Let us appreciate at this point the famous analogy of the poor man and the millionaire, from the *Lotus Sutra*. It is a wonderful parallel to our practice, and also to how enlightenment should be pursued and finally achieved and deepened. First of all, the son of a millionaire leaves his father's home and starts wandering. This father's house with its limitless wealth is the house of the Buddha, our own house. In other words, at some point we left the home of our true self.

Soon the son becomes poor and in his travels experiences all sorts of pain and suffering, difficulty and trouble, while his father spends year after year worrying about his son and searching for him. Finally, after many years spent wandering around, the son happens to appear in front of the very house where he was raised, but it's been so long he can't even recognize it. In fact, such a huge, gorgeous house frightens him, yet he is curious and starts looking around.

Then his father happens to see him, and even though the son has changed quite a bit, the father immediately recognizes him and sends his servants to take him in. But seeing people coming out from the gate and approaching him, the son thinks they've come to catch him because he's been hanging around, and he starts to run away. The messengers go back and report this to the father, and ask, "Should we grab him and bring him in or not?" The father says, "No, don't go after him. We'll have someone dressed the way he is go after him and tell him, 'The boss of that house is a very kind man. We are working there, and he wants you to come and work with us. You don't need to worry about where to stay and what to eat.'" Then the son finally agrees, and though still afraid, enters the house.

Relating again to our practice, we have many people who come in and out. Those who are still suspicious about our practice could be compared to the son at this point. But anyway, coming in and starting to sit parallels starting to work in that home.

Then the father gradually promotes his son's position. This again relates to our practice. We practice year after year using all kinds of gimmicks. I shouldn't say gimmicks, but in a way, expedient means such as koans are gimmicks. Then we improve ourselves little by little. By doing zazen, we make ourselves stronger and stronger. Then after years of work there, he establishes his position quite nicely, just as, after years of practice, we establish ourselves quite firmly, quite steadily. His father even asks him to take care of all financial statements, putting him in charge of practically everything. But still the son doesn't consider that all those treasures, those possessions, are his own; still they seem like someone else's. Finally, when the time really ripens and the son is ready to accept practically anything, the father reveals the truth, but by this time it is no surprise for the son at all. That moment can be compared to the moment of enlightenment. Prior to that time, the son must have been aware of progressing to higher positions, of becoming more and more confident and more and more capable of dealing with people and handling things.

But again, even succeeding to the position of overseer is not quite sufficient. Attaining enlightenment is not quite sufficient. What is necessary? Again, our path is wonderfully paralleled by how the master of a big family is supposed to behave. For example, the one who acts bossy is not really the boss. Penetrating into that position, digesting all sorts of things, one becomes more and more subdued, more understanding, more sympathetic. Then finally, one becomes fully mature as the master. The same is true of our practice. After attaining enlightenment or after succeeding to the Dharma, we are still green in a way. We have to grow further and further, until eventually all our rough or glaring qualities are subdued, and we really become one with the whole family, the whole society. Then we are truly the master; then our practice, our life, is truly accomplished.

Now let's look at a poem by Dogen Zenji entitled "The Lotus Sutra":

> When you grasp
> The heart of this sutra
> Even the voices
> Of selling and buying in the marketplace
> Expound the Dharma.

"When [we really] grasp the heart of this sutra. . . " "Heart" could also be translated as "mind." "When you grasp the mind of this sutra, even the voices of selling and buying in the marketplace expound the Dharma." He's referring not only to "the voices of selling and buying in the marketplace." The sounds of cars passing in the street, birds chirping in the backyard, dogs barking, kids yelling, helicopters buffeting the wind overhead, all are nothing but "expounding the Dharma."

How do we grasp the mind of this sutra? In the *Diamond Sutra* (*Vajracchedika*) there is the expression, "All buddhas and buddhas' teachings arise from this sutra." What is this sutra? It's muji*. And to see this sutra is kensho. "This sutra" is Buddha-nature, true self, or whatever you name it. In the *Diamond Sutra* there is another famous passage: "If one tries to see the Tathagata (Buddha) through forms and voices, he cannot see the Tathagata." Again, what does that mean? If we try to see it, we can't see it. In a way, this is a dilemma we are practicing to overcome. When we are something else, the seer and the seen are separate, there is a subject-object relationship; that's how the common level of consciousness works. It's not that dichotomy or dualism itself is wrong. In a way everything is dualistic—enlightenment and delusion; heaven and earth; man and woman; husband and wife; parents and children; teacher and student; right and left; right and wrong; night and day; ignorance and wisdom—it's all there. The point is that we should transcend that dichotomy and see the essential unity.

We have koans such as "delusion is enlightenment; life and death are nirvana itself." How can life and death be nirvana? Life and death are samsara, which is the opposite of nirvana. Or Sengai's haiku:

> Old pond
> Basho jumps in
> The sound of water

Physically, Basho doesn't jump in. Then what does it mean? Somehow we have to come back to the conscious sphere. One description of Zen is, "Zen is the name for the mind, the mind is the body of Zen." What is this mind? When we understand this mind, we understand Zen.

Bankei Zenji was a Japanese Rinzai master who lived about 250 years ago, and was a contemporary and friend of one of the patriarchs in our lineage, Tenkei Denson Zenji. One day Bankei Zenji said to a group of people, "You are here to listen to my talk and I am talking to you. You should understand what I tell you. What is this mind? A dog is barking outside. When you hear that dog, you are not trying to do anything; you just perceive it. That is the mind of the Buddha." It is so true. Without trying to do anything, we are living quite satisfactorily. We see something; we naturally respond to it. We hear something; we naturally respond to it. We do something; we naturally just do it. Then there is no problem. In other words, let consciousness work as consciousness. But somehow we always add something extra to it, and this generates problems. In a sense, our practice is to trim off these extra things.

Zen Master Wu-men Hui-k'ai (Mumon Ekai) advises those working on muji to trim off all false knowledge and awareness, and really put themselves into it. Dogen Zenji says the same thing: "Try to cut off the root of consciousness." In other words, become plainly, genuinely yourself. Such a state is often compared to a mirror. Explaining the passage in the *Heart Sutra*, "Not stained, not pure," Master Bankei says that a mirror just reflects a dog's droppings, and when we remove those droppings, no stain is left on the mirror. Then it reflects a beautiful flower, and when we remove it, no purity is left. "Not stained, not pure." He says the same thing of "no increase, no decrease." A heavy thing is reflected on the mirror, but no heavy thing remains. No light thing, no big thing, no small thing remains; "no increase, no decrease." That's what's called "no mind" or "no self." If we make ourselves really open, and unconditioned by any ideas or standards, right there we can live quite nicely.

I am reminded of the famous passage by Dogen Zenji: "To study the self is to forget the self," which means to make ourselves into a clear mirror. Then, being so, we can reflect everything as it is, we can "be enlightened by all things." No division exists, just unity and harmony. But such harmony or unity shouldn't be static. It should work. And how does it work? Sometimes the practice of Zen is compared to climbing a mountain. Without climbing to the top of the mountain, not only can't we really understand how splendid it is to stand on the mountain peak, but also we can't know how wonderful and also how difficult it is to climb to the top. And of course, at the beginning, we start from some place which is our own home. The top of the mountain could be compared to the accomplishment of enlightenment; staying there is static and useless, a big trap, so we have to come down. In the *Surangama Sutra*, fifty *makyo** are listed, and the worst makyo is to think that you have accomplished enough.

When we open our *oryoki** to eat a meal, first we put the spoon on the left side, facing up, which means ascending, accomplishing our practice, acquiring Buddha's wisdom. Then, after finishing the meal, we place the spoon to the right, facing down, which means descending, loving, caring, having compassion and affection. We have to climb down the mountain to share its delight with other people and encourage them to climb up the mountain of enlightenment. So first we start from the home which is ourself. As Dogen Zenji says, "To study Buddhism is to study the self." That's our starting point. "To forget the self is to be enlightened by all things." After attaining enlightenment we must then further utilize that wisdom as compassion. That's what Dogen Zenji means when he says: "This traceless enlightenment is continued endlessly." In other words, seeing everything and everybody as part of ourselves, we take good care of them. I would especially like to emphasize the importance of taking care; each of us should really make this his or her practice. Regardless of how much or how little we accomplish, whatever we do we are using both wisdom and compassion. That's what I want you to be really aware of.

The different stages that we can achieve are endless. For example, Master Tung-shan Liang-chieh (Tozan Ryokai) divides them into five different stages. Or we have six oxherding pictures, or ten oxherding pictures. Just as after climbing the mountain we come back down and return home, so in the ten oxherding pictures there is the sixth stage, "riding on the ox returning home." The tenth stage is, as you know, going into the marketplace to do whatever is necessary. Selling and buying is nothing but the manifestation of the Dharma.

Then why is it necessary to help or to save other people? It is important to understand how our life goes. From the intrinsic standpoint we can say all of us are buddhas, but somehow we aren't really satisfied that this is true. We have to actually experience it, really see how true it is by ourselves. But even seeing it is not enough; we have to practice continuously. That's what Dogen Zenji calls the spiral of continuous practice. How do we let it continue? By raising the bodhi mind, practicing, achieving enlightenment and attaining nirvana. Practice goes on in this way forever.

Amitabha Buddha said, "Until everybody is enlightened, I won't enter into perfect nirvana." In the *Vimalakirti Nirdesa Sutra*, the layman Vimalakirti says, "I am sick because people are sick." And in the Rinzai school, we use the koan, Master Po-yün's (Hakuun's) "not yet, not enough." However much we accomplish, still it's insufficient, incomplete. So what is enlightenment?

Soen Nakagawa Roshi composed a haiku at the beginning of the year of the Dragon (1976) which I thought might be a nice way to end this chapter on enlightenment:

> Ascend the slope
> Descend that very slope
> Spring of the dragon.

Daiun Sogaku Harada (1870–1961)

TWO

Approaches to Enlightenment

Daiun Harada Roshi
Translated by Kohun Yamada Roshi
and Paul Shepard

Introduction

Even though Zen is fashionable at the present time, if asked what Zen is, not many would be able to answer with clarity and certainty. And even if they could answer, they would answer by taking only two or three waves of the sea of Zen for the whole of Zen. Some others think of irresoluteness or dissoluteness or self-indulgence as Zen. There are even extreme cases of those who consider their own egoistic views and attachments to be Zen. They seem to mistake one of those practices, one of those "waves"—working on koans; just becoming one with sitting; contemplating benevolence or counting the breath—for the whole of Zen.

We must know that there are hundreds and thousands of ways of Zen. All the preachings of the Buddha during his whole life are the teachings of Zen. The eighty-thousand Dharma-gates are all the active means of Zen. Penetrating into the core of the meaning of the world is called Zen, but those who are captured by words are called the teachers of no wisdom. The first thing we should do is to have a general view of Zen and be mindful not to take what is not Zen for Zen, or to mistake one part of Zen for the whole.

Quiet Meditative Zen

Now, though we usually say simply *Zen*, there are many kinds of Zen: ordinary man's Zen, Hinayana Zen, Zen of other religions besides Buddhism, Mahayana Zen, and supreme Zen transmitted rightly from Buddhas and Patriarchs. They are different from each other in depth or shallowness, breadth or narrowness, largeness or smallness, right or wrong and good or bad. It should not be forgotten that even though there are so many kinds of Zen, *quiet meditative Zen* is really the root of all Zen. Quiet meditative Zen is to become still and quiet. It is to unify one's spirit and mind, to enter the state of no-self, and to achieve complete stillness and peace through and through. In this Zen, there is no difference in depth or shallowness, breadth or narrowness. In the extremity of this Zen one can enter the state of no-consciousness for one year, for ten years, or for a limitless period of time.

Meditative Zen is the fundamental Way that everyone must actually practice, whether he has no religion at all or is of another religion, whether he believes in the Buddha-nature or not, whether he knows about the law of cause and effect or not, whether he is a military man, an educator or a businessman. From the Buddhist point of view, this Zen is called *ordinary man's Zen, samadhi of the three worlds*, or *secular Zen*.

For the sake of convenience, I will explain this Zen, classifying it into three kinds: *meditation Zen, no-consciousness Zen* and *no-attachment Zen*. In meditation Zen one takes up some words from the sutras or the records of the teachings of the Patriarchs, or the watchwords of ancient wise men, and sitting quietly, savors these words or ponders them. Through these means one works on bringing the mind to concentration. Christian prayer and Fujita's method of quiet sitting may be considered types of this kind of Zen.

No-consciousness Zen is to arrive at the state of no-thinking through various methods. In no-attachment Zen one does not meditate, does not desire the state of no-thinking, but only sits in complete oneness. It is the fundamental Zen of Buddhism. It is all right either with koans or without koans. But that which we wish to attain here is only quiet sitting, nothing else. To say that it brings about self-composure is a negative way of expressing it. If we say it in a positive way, we can say that the more we become composed, the more peaceful our inner world naturally becomes, harmonizing with the virtue of self-nature little by little, though we are not aware of it.

Delusion-and-Realization Zen

This kind of Zen is practiced by those people whose inner world has naturally become peaceful and tranquil, and the waves of dualistic consciousness and feelings do not move disturbingly anymore. Furthermore, because they have often heard that all human beings are endowed with Buddha-nature, they have naturally come to believe in this and have aroused the determination to realize it clearly by all means.

Therefore, the Zen which they are going to practice is not merely the secular, relative Zen. It is the Zen by which one turns from the profane and enters into the sacred, the practice by which one turns from delusions to enlightenment. It is not the secular Dharma in the least, but the Zen which is totally peculiar to the Buddha-Dharma.

For the sake of convenience, I will divide this kind of Zen into three levels: *proximate Zen, gradual-enlightenment Zen* and *sudden-enlightenment Zen*.

In proximate Zen one already knows that there is the great fact of the essential world and wants to turn from the ordinary to enter into the holy. As the practice proceeds, the state of consciousness becomes ripe and pure, and, though in a hazy way, begins to come in contact with the light of the essential world. In such a way, the world of oneness appears in a "proximate" fashion. (It is not yet the real thing.) This proximate Zen corresponds to the so-called "proximate level" of the Tendai Sect.

In this level of Zen there are two kinds: with koan, and without koan. In the latter, when one faithfully follows the instruction of the master and continues to sit earnestly, persevering without interruption, one comes to a point where one naturally achieves a state that resembles being one with the Dharma-body. But this is where one is apt to fall into *buji* Zen (Zen without enlightenment).

In koan Zen, one is first given an old koan, and biting it sideways and up and down, looking at it, and thinking about it many times in the wrong way, one falls into a tight spot. Then, unconsciously, one suddenly attains a bit of experience: "Oh, it's probably this!" And so one passes that koan with a slight feeling of joy. After that, one by one, he passes fifty, a hundred or two hundred koans. In this way, a kind of proximate Zen is achieved.

Let me speak here of the good and bad points of koan Zen and no-koan Zen. In no-koan Zen, the power of concentration (*joriki*) is sufficient but it lacks intellect. In koan Zen, the intellect is sufficient, but it is lacking in the power of concentration. For example, no-koan Zen is like having feet without sight, and koan Zen is like having eyes without strength in the feet.

In gradual-enlightenment Zen, with or without koans, one enters into the deep absorption of becoming one, and sits persistently for one to ten years. Then, when the time comes, all of a sudden the real joy of piercing thoroughly to the bottom manifests itself. Here, the master will approve half of it, and giving the disciple many koans, will polish the degree of his state of consciousness for some time. Then, at his own discretion, the master will choose the right time and will not allow the disciple to pass, but will bring him once again to the "great death" and then to the great enlightened life, causing him finally to pass the last and hardest barrier.

This kind of Zen practice, though it makes the disciple work on koans, is completely different from proximate Zen, which is a kind of conceptual Zen. It is not Zen of the' head, but Zen of the whole body down to the very toes. It manifests itself when a person really becomes one with the koan and the time is sufficiently ripe. This Zen does not need to use the head in the slightest. In this way, it progresses step by step. This is where Hakuin's twelve great enlightenments and the eighteen great enlightenments of Hsüeh-feng (Seppo) appeared.

Sudden-enlightenment Zen is not the way of gradual progression. It is the Zen which leads the disciple to enter the land of the Tathagata directly, in one leap. During ten, twenty, or thirty years of practice, even if there may be some degree of realization of the Way, the master disregards it as makyo, and the practicer also does not rejoice in it. There is no looking aside until the very marrow is reached. Until the last true home is attained, various steps are not approved, everything along the way being thoroughly killed. Yen-t'ou's (Ganto's) final treatment of Hsüeh-feng, Yün-men's (Ummon's) fifteen years of dealing with attendant Yüan (En), and Shoju Rojin's handling of Hakuin are examples of this type of Zen. [2]

These days, however, there is not one master who is kind enough to use such poisonous means. Even if there were, I don't think there is a practitioner who would have a strong enough constitution to submit willingly to such obliging means. It is most deplorable that the garden of our Patriarchs has been desolated to such an extent. However, there are still masters and students of gradual-enlightenment Zen. If one breaks through the final and most difficult barrier gradually, the essence of the experience is no different from that of sudden-enlightenment Zen.

Self-nature Zen

Self-nature Zen is also called self-nature samadhi Zen, the Zen of essentiality or the Buddha's supreme Zen. This is the Zen of a person who has accomplished the Zen of "turning from the ordinary and entering into the holy" and whose enlightened eye is perfect and clear. This, too, is easier to explain by dividing it into three classes: the period of stinking of the Dharma; the period of no-stench; and the period of transcendence. The first, the period of stinking of the Dharma, is the period when one is extremely happy. It is like gaining a lamp on a dark night, or like a beggar all of a sudden becoming rich. He is so full of joy that he doesn't know his hands and feet are dancing by themselves. Daitsu Chisho (Mahabhijna Jnanabhibhu) Buddha's sitting in the zendo for ten kalpas, Shakyamuni's twenty-one days of meditation, and Te-shan's (Tokusan's) visiting Kuei-shan (Isan), all show the symptoms of the illness of this period.[3]

In the second period of no-stench, the stinking of the Dharma embodied in the dancing for joy or in the suffering which comes when actual life does not coincide with the enlightened eye disappears. At last one is at ease and has reached the stage of "the merit of no-merit." But here, too, one does not escape from the partial stench of the Dharma. It might have been at this stage that Kuei-shan, at the age of seventy-three, said, "Just recently, I have come to real peace in my heart," or that Hakuin, at the age of seventy, realized that he had returned home and was sitting calmly.

The third stage, the period of transcendence, is the time when consciousness of enlightenment is actually transcended. Of course delusion and enlightenment as well as life and death in the slowly changing world are totally transcended. The stage of discussing delusion or enlightenment, Buddha or sentient-being, is passed over, and one completely becomes an ordinary person. This is what is called the "great person of immeasurable worth." It is called the supreme stage of Buddha, or the state of consciousness of the Buddha.

Previously I spoke of the three classifications of Zen as quiet meditative Zen, delusion-and-realization Zen and self-nature Zen. Quiet meditative Zen is the root and basis of all Zen. It is the elemental Zen that must be practiced once in order to enter the Zen of Buddhism.

Now the proximate-Zen master gives koans immediately to those who have not yet cultivated the root and can't even believe in the principle of Buddha-nature or the law of causation. So it does not amount to anything and is only harmful, profiting no one.

Zen which converts delusion into realization is the period of awakening in Buddhism, namely, Zen which takes realization as the most important principle. And self-nature Zen is, we may say, Zen which realizes truly and perfectly the intrinsically awakened nature.

In quiet meditative Zen there are the three periods of: quiet meditation, no-thoughts and no-attachment.

In the Zen which converts delusion into realization there are three classes: proximate Zen, gradual-enlightenment Zen and sudden-enlightenment Zen.

In self-nature Zen there are also three periods: stinking of the Dharma, no-stench and transcendence.

Thus my explanation divides the three kinds of Zen into three groups each, giving us nine in all. Even in quiet meditative Zen there is a beginning, middle and end, and the levels of depth and shallowness among them are, in some cases, as different as a star from the sun.

In the Zen which converts delusion into realization, too, the difference between the beginning and the end cannot even be compared to the difference between clouds and mud. And it is impossible to compare the differences which exist in the beginning, middle, and end stages of self-nature Zen to anything. As to the ability of practitioners, there are actually ten thousand or one hundred thousand different levels, and accordingly the number of classifications in Zen is measureless.

There are persons, however, who are still in an elementary period of Zen practice, but straightaway force their way into the practice of the Zen which converts delusion into realization, or even worse, immediately begin indiscriminately to follow the Way of self-nature Zen. Because of this, the true Dharma becomes a false Dharma and the Buddha-Dharma becomes meaningless. Tell me, you people of today who practice Zen so recklessly, do you understand the true spirit of Buddha who did not disclose the true reality for forty years?[4]

When the guidance of the master corresponds fittingly to the level of the practitioner, every Zen emits the light of the Buddha, but if the guidance is not fit for the practitioner, any dharma is no longer Dharma. I can only sigh deeply when I see that nowadays there are too many proximate-Zen masters who are haphazardly teaching only proximate Zen or the Zen of samadhi of self-nature, regardless of the levels of the practitioners. Isn't there any master who wants to cultivate by practice the eye-power of the wisdom of subtle observation?

Although the three kinds of Zen each have three classifications, resulting in nine separate classes, each one can be found in all the others. Quiet meditative Zen permeates through both delusion-and-realization Zen and self-nature Zen. Delusion-and-realization Zen permeates through both quiet meditative Zen and self-nature Zen.

And even the marvelous state of self-nature Zen is completely present in the other two types of Zen. So actually, the nine classes, each containing nine, could be multiplied by nine to make eighty-one classifications. And if we consider the various levels of depth and shallowness in each class, we realize that there are hundreds and even thousands of degrees.

But even though there are hundreds and thousands of classes, there is just one pure Great Way that penetrates them all. This penetrating Great Way is called the *king samadhi of no-rank*. In this stage it is said that the practice of beginners is not other than the whole body of intrinsic realization. It is also called the sitting seat in one's own home. In other words, it is becoming completely one, entrusting oneself composedly to the course of things. I will deal with the details of this Great Way in the next section.

The Great Way of Permeating Oneness

Earlier, I explained roughly that in quiet meditative Zen, the waves of delusive consciousness and feelings are stilled. In the Zen which converts delusion into enlightenment, the root of consciousness is broken, delusions are cut away and one is allowed to enter into the essential world. In self-nature Zen, one rests peacefully in the king samadhi, enjoying it by oneself and continuing the practice on one's own while saving others eternally. However, one may mistakenly stick to the various classes of depth and shallowness and forget that from beginning to end there is nothing but the *Great Way of permeating oneness*. For fear of this happening, I will explain here about the Great Way.

The Great Way of permeating oneness is that all living beings are intrinsically Buddha, that all living beings are emancipated from the beginning. It is just that because of delusions and discriminative concepts it is hard to recognize this fact. A man of old has said that beyond the elimination of ordinary, delusive consciousness, there is no sacred realization. Therefore, the main point in Zen is to just get rid of these delusive consciousnesses, that is, to become completely naked, to become completely one, to experience the "great death." Even though there are incomparable differences in depth and shallowness from the beginning of quiet meditation to the end of self-nature, it is a depth and shallowness of the state of consciousness, not the depth and shallowness of Zen itself. Zen is the one Dharma which penetrates through from the beginning to the end. What is this one Dharma? It is just the great death, just the great nakedness, just becoming completely one. This becoming one is as necessary for the enlightened person who is practicing self-nature Zen as for the beginner who is working on quiet meditative Zen.

It follows, therefore, that although there are hundreds and thousands of means in Zen, the main point of it is merely *just sitting*. The content of the eighty-four thousand good expedients is nothing other than becoming one. This becoming one is not only the essential element for entering the Way but in fact the Great Way itself. This is called "the classless treasury of the true Dharma eye, the marvelous mind of nirvana," or "this living Fact." Believing in this classless Zen and at the same time not forgetting the Zen of classes, believing in the Zen of classes yet not forgetting classless Zen, we need a firm belief in the marvelous subtlety with which they mutually intermingle. If one can grasp them and let them go at the proper time, thus being able to treat accordingly those practitioners who come from the four directions of the world, one will be called an immeasurably enlightened Zen person, who has the skillful hand which kills and gives life freely and can save donkey or horse with ease.[5]

THREE

What Is Enlightenment?: Dharma Dialogue

with Tetsugen Glassman Sensei

As you all know, the word *Buddha* means "awakened one," "enlightened one." Buddhism is a religion, a way of life, of awakening or of enlightenment. When he attained enlightenment, Shakyamuni Buddha exclaimed: "How wonderful, how wonderful! Each one of us, every sentient being, is the Buddha, is enlightenment, without exception." Each one of us here is enlightened, is the Buddha.

Now I'd like to ask you, "What is enlightenment?"

Q: Enlightenment is the three poisons: greed, anger and ignorance. Greed: the desire to enlighten all beings.
Sensei: Anger?
Q: Anger: anger at delusion. Ignorance: just don't know. Just don't know and keep that "don't know."
Sensei: Thank you for your answer.
Q: Thank you.

Q: Enlightenment is wondering whether my V.U. meters are deflecting, whether this microphone (*taps mike three times*) is working. Enlightenment is watching your toes and your fingers wiggle when you tell us that every one of us is enlightened.
Sensei: Tell me, why do we practice? (*Pause*) Thank you for your answer.

Q: When I came here about four months ago it was because I felt that I didn't know anything, and now I feel I know less and less.
Sensei: Definitely, that's a good way to start, but also we have to know, so let's keep working together. Thank you.

Q: I think enlightenment is loving all people.
Sensei: Shakyamuni Buddha said each one of us, everything as it is, is enlightened, is the Buddha. You're making distinctions. What is enlightenment?
Q: I was going to say "nothing." But then I thought about it and I didn't think that was the right answer. I don't know.
Sensei: Thank you for your answer.

Q: I don't know what enlightenment is, but it seems to me that to live an enlightened life is not to be partial to oneself.
Sensei: What do you mean by that?
Q: I think that if one were not partial to oneself, one would not be separated from anything, and I feel very strongly that, as Dogen Zenji says, one would then be enlightened by all things.
Sensei: It's interesting. When we take the vows as Buddhists, have jukai, we take sixteen precepts*. One way of looking at these precepts is called "Buddha-nature," to see the precepts as aspects of the enlightened nature. There is also a Mahayana way and a Hinayana way of looking at these precepts. Of course, each one of us probably has a different view, but in Buddhism there are three standard ways. From the standpoint of Buddha-nature, as soon as a distinction arises between ourselves and others, we violate the precepts.

The seventh precept is, "Don't elevate yourself by criticizing others." From the standpoint of Buddha-nature, as soon as you separate yourself from others, right there you are elevating yourself by criticizing others. The only way not to do that is to eliminate that distinction, which is very difficult. Always when something goes wrong we don't look at ourselves. Instead, we say, "It's his fault. It's their fault. Look what they're doing to me. Look how sloppy he is in his work. Look how jealous she is. Look how lazy he is."

Last night I was sitting with my wife and eight-year-old son. We were talking in the living room together and he started whimpering. My wife said to him, "Tell me what's wrong. We'll talk about it." He said, "There's only one person that can make it better." "Who's that?" she asked. "Me," he answered. That "me" is what we have to see; that's everything. So in a way, be partial to yourself, but see that self without distinguishing between this and that, yourself and others. Just Self. Then be partial to that. Thank you.

Q: (*Comes up, says nothing, takes a picture of Sensei,* [p. 22] *and leaves.*)

Q: Sensei, I used to have big ideas that one day I'd be enlightened, but I don't really think about that anymore. It's just a wonder in each moment. I can include in that my own anger, ignorance, all the dumb things I and other people do; it's all fine. Or rather, it is fine and it isn't fine. Either way, I think it's just being awake each moment. Of course, I'm not awake each moment, but it seems to me as practice goes on that the amount of time one is able to stay awake increases, at least a little bit. I just want to keep practicing. I don't have any ideas anymore.

Sensei: It's interesting, though. A synonym for *enlightened* is *awake*. You said that you don't think about enlightenment any more, but you're trying to be awake a little bit more each time.

Q: I think that just happens. I don't mean to say I sit trying to make it happen. I think that just sitting, going to dokusan*. . .

Sensei: Please remember, not being awake is still enlightenment.

Q: Yes, I know. I understand that, and somehow I just don't think about any of this anymore. I used to spend all my time thinking about it.

Sensei: We ought to learn to play chess together.

Q: That's right. Thank you.

Q: Sensei, I pretty much agree with what I've heard people say about enlightenment, the unity with all things, with all beings. But the actual experience of it I couldn't describe.

Sensei: At all times, it is just this unity which we're experiencing.

Q: Then why do we seek outside? What are we seeking for?

Sensei: *Don't* seek outside of it. Joan takes tea; if she makes a mistake the tea teacher slaps her hand with a fan. If we seek outside of it we should slap our hands with a fan. But we'll keep making mistakes and we'll keep seeking for it outside of ourselves. Why? (*Pause*) Thank you.

Q: Hi. How are you?

Sensei: Fine. How are you?

Q: Good, fine.

Sensei: You're always fine.

Q: Yes. Are you?

Sensei: Nope.

Q: What do you do about it?

Sensei: Well, it depends. (*laughter*)

Q: Because I'm not fine sometimes, too.

Sensei: That means we're human. There's nothing wrong with that. It's good to be human. (*Pause*) Why is it good to be human?

Q: Because we are. It's a fact.

Sensei: Let me ask you something. Why don't you like *shosan* (Dharma dialogue)?

Q: (*Laughs*) I don't?

Sensei: (*Laughs*)

Q: I like *you*.

Sensei: I'm not shosan. I'm *shosanshi* (shosan leader). (*Laughter*)

Q: What? Excuse me, why don't I like shosan?

Sensei: Yes.

Q: I do.

Sensei: Why do you like it?

Q: Why do I like it? You know, I neither like it nor dislike it.

Sensei: Okay, what is enlightenment?

Q: Sitting here talking to you.

Sensei: Thank you.

Q: I guess it's being able to experience that there's no one out there.

Sensei: What do you mean by "no one out there?"

Q: That everything that occurs, like being here now, is created right here in me. I create any attachment or illusion that I have. There is nothing different out there.

Sensei: We could say that, but that's just one side. There *is* something out there. We have to see both sides. In fact, we have to see all sides. But first we start with the hard one: there is nothing out there. After we see what that really means, then we have to see that there is something out there. Let's keep working on that together.

Q: Thank you.

Q: Sensei, enlightenment is realizing that the attainment of enlightenment and all goals in life are not important, and that you shouldn't go beyond this moment.

Sensei: Do you realize that?

Q: No.

Sensei: It's a very simple statement. Why don't you realize it?

Q: I'm not enlightened.

Sensei: Shakyamuni Buddha says you are. I say you are.

Q: I don't understand that I am yet.

Sensei: Okay, we'll work on that. Thank you.

Q: I feel like you're an old friend.

Sensei: I think so.

Q: I was going to say that I don't know what enlightenment is but I know what delusion is. Delusion is getting up and going to the NBC carpentry shop every day and working ten or thirteen hours every day and getting big paychecks.

Sensei: One of our famous koans is: delusion is enlightenment.

Q: That's why I said that.

Sensei: Thank you.

Q: Enlightenment is myself but I don't know what that is.

Sensei: Enlightenment is myself but I don't know what that is. (*Pause*) That was my answer. Thank you.

Q: I also don't know what enlightenment is. But perhaps when I reach that state I'll be able to deal with my embarrassment a little bit better. And perhaps I'll be in a state of mind where I'm not always creating my own problems.

Sensei: Or you'll be realizing that you are the one who is always creating your problems. Thank you.

Q: Sensei, enlightenment is learning how to take care of ourselves, and learning that taking care of ourselves is taking care of everyone.

Sensei: Even further, we can drop the word "learning," and just put our effort into taking care. Thank you.

Q: Sensei, I don't know. Enlightenment is knowing that something is and is not at the same time?

Sensei: That sounds tricky.

Q: That's what you told me the last time. (*Laughter*)

Sensei: "Something is and something is not at the same time."

It's more. It's "something *is* and something is *not*." See the difference? *At the same time.* And that's why we practice. As long as we have the slightest confusion, the slightest uncertainty, we have to get rid of it. Why? (*Pause*) Thank you.

Q: Sensei, I don't understand what enlightenment is either. When I was a research scientist I used to think that I understood things. I would do experiments and find out answers but the answers would just present more problems. So I'm not sure if it's really necessary to understand things, at least in the sense of analyzing them. But it's simply amazing to me that we can do experiments, and that we can practice, and that we can be enlightened. But as you say, there are still things that we have to take care of.

Sensei: Yes, koans are experiments. We work on koans in the same way that we do experiments: to learn about something, to find out what something is. We could say right from the beginning that it's all ridiculous, we don't need koans to find out that we are just as we are. We don't need koans to find out that we are Buddha, we can just realize it directly. We don't need experiments to know that light lights up the room. So why do we experiment? Why do we work on koans? To find out, to clarify, and to keep on going.

There's a verse in the *Blue Cliff Record*: "Mountains heaped upon mountains and clouds heaped upon clouds." That's our practice. You climb a mountain and you see higher mountains. When you've climbed those mountains, you see higher mountains, and beyond those higher mountains, you see clouds. And clouds are heaped upon clouds, and upon that is heaped the vast empty sky. That's our practice. Let's keep going. Thank you.

Q: Sensei, I'm worried that I don't have anything to say. Sometimes I'm worried that I have too much to say.

Sensei: Put your mind at ease. Thank you.

Q: I think that everybody's wrong when they say that it all happens at once. Because I'd like it to be happening little by little all the time. I suppose what they mean is that you suddenly realize that it's happened.

Sensei: Always the insights and realizations happen all at once, but experience and growth are gradual. You can't have an insight gradually. It's like shooting an arrow at a target. When you hit the bull's-eye, it happens instantaneously; it just hits it. But practicing with the bow, placing the target, all those things happen gradually. How do you split them apart? (*Pause*) You can't. I answered it. Thank you.

Q: Sensei, about a month ago I started jogging in the morning. Actually I started getting ready to jog and spent most of the first three weeks walking. Now I'm beginning to jog a little bit more, maybe a third of the time jogging and two thirds of the time walking. The other day when I was adding one more level of jogging to my practice, in that exercise period I pulled a muscle in my left leg and so I had to stop jogging and walk for a while and then rub the muscle to relax the spasm. When I get home in the mornings from that running/walking I've usually worked up quite a sweat, so I take a shower and clean up and get ready to go to work.
Sensei: Thank you.

Q: I think that enlightenment is never being bored, and especially never being bored when you're helping other people because everyone is the same, so helping someone else is just helping yourself.
Sensei: Being bored is enlightenment.
Q: It doesn't feel very enlightened. (*Laughter*)
Sensei: Being bored, loving everyone; one is, one is not.

Q: Sensei, being enlightened is finding out who you are and liking what you find and therefore liking everything you find around you.
Sensei: Stop at the first sentence.
Q: Finding out who you are?
Sensei: That's enough. That's enough. Thank you.

Q: Sensei, I don't know what enlightenment is. I guess I hope it means smiling inside, rather than screaming.
Sensei: I hope so too. But sometimes it's necessary to scream. Thank you.

Q: Sensei, enlightenment is enlightenment.
Sensei: That's a cop-out.
Q: I said too much.
Sensei: Okay, thanks.

Q: Everything is as it is.
Sensei: Is everybody happy?

Q: They don't have to be.

Sensei: Satisfied?

Q: No, and that's as it is, too.

Sensei: Is there any difference between your understanding of enlightenment and that of Shakyamuni Buddha?

Q: Yes.

Sensei: What?

Q: I don't experience it the way he experienced it.

Sensei: How do you know how he experienced it?

Q: I don't know. I just read some things that I don't understand and I'm not satisfied with what happens when I read them. That's why I practice.

Sensei: Then let's practice.

Q: Thank you for your answer.

Q: Sensei, at this moment, for me, just this moment.

Sensei: In a way we can't say more. The only change I would make to that is: just this moment is *just* this moment. Thank you.

Q: Sensei, I don't know what enlightenment is, but I will continue to practice because it feels good. I love it and I hate it.

Sensei: And it hurts the legs sometimes and it hurts the back sometimes.

Q: Yes, but I love it.

Sensei: And it soothes the mind sometimes. And I guarantee if you keep practicing you'll come up and you'll say, "I know what enlightenment is."

Q: Thank you very much.

Sensei: Thank you. But please find out for yourself. Don't depend on anybody else.

Q: Sensei, I don't know if I know what it is. It could be called anything or everything. In my understanding, it's being able to see into the void, to see that there's always something in the void, the void in your own mind.

Sensei: Yes, seeing what's in the void. We chant the *Heart Sutra* every morning and we say: "form is emptiness; emptiness is form." We have to see that void, "emptiness;" we have to see what's in the void, "form;" and we have to see that form and emptiness are the same thing, and that it's all in here (*tapping himself on the head with his stick*), it's all in here. Thank you.

Q: Sensei, enlightenment is the doubt that kneels here now, I doubt it.
Sensei: We need doubt to keep going. We need determination to eliminate that doubt. Let's work together on both of those.

Q: Sensei, I'm not going to tell you what enlightenment is. (*Laughter*) It's not funny. I mean it's funny, but there's a reason for that.
Sensei: Because you're mean. (*Laughter*)
Q: Sometimes I am, that's enlightenment. I'm dissatisfied with my knowledge of what enlightenment is. That's why I practice and that's enlightenment.
Sensei: Thank you.

Q: Sensei, I don't know what enlightenment is, but why does it take so long?
Sensei: It doesn't.
Q: Realizing it seems to.
Sensei: Actually there's one simple answer.
Q: What's that?
Sensei: You should know.
Q: I was reading. . .
Sensei: No, you should know.
Q: I don't.
Sensei: Find out.

Q: I was going to say, "enlightenment is being the last one in line," but somebody stepped behind me. So it's being the next to the last one in line.
Sensei: We all can't be next to the last. But we're all enlightened. Thank you.

Sensei: Now I'm going to get it. (*Laughter*)
Q: "Enlightenment is being the last one in line."
Everyday is a new day; every moment is a new moment. Sometimes I'm very sad and I don't know why. Some days I feel very alive and intelligent and I don't know why. And I used to think that enlightenment was trying to embrace all of those moments in some way, to make some effort to include them all, but that's become totally impossible.
Sensei: Thank you.

Enlightenment. Not an easy subject. Shakyamuni Buddha said that all of us, not just humans but all of us, as we are, are Buddha. There's a cushion over there; it's enlightened. What does that mean? It's deluded. What does that mean? What are its delusions? How is it enlightened? In a way, looking at the cushion might be a little easier than looking at ourselves. We're so complex. The word *enlightenment*, the word *delusion*, they're extra. What is that cushion? "Things are what they are." That's a simple statement. Whether we have an insight or not, things are what they are. Always the insight comes (*snaps his fingers*), but our body, our memory, and our brain are based on wonderful mechanisms which, whether they see something or not, have their own residual way of operating. We're affected by our insights, but not like (*snaps his fingers again*), and so we have sudden and gradual enlightenment.

Always the realization is the easy part. Actualizing the realization is the hard part, which is why we say it takes ten, twenty, thirty, forty, fifty years of practice to know what enlightenment is, to really know what it is in the bones and the marrow. When Hakuin Zenji was in his seventies, having had maybe a dozen major enlightenment experiences and innumerable minor ones, he said that he was finally getting to the point where his body was acting in accord with the way that he saw things. We practice, and in a way we can say there's no need to practice. The cushion's the cushion. I am what I am. But that's not enough. Thank you.

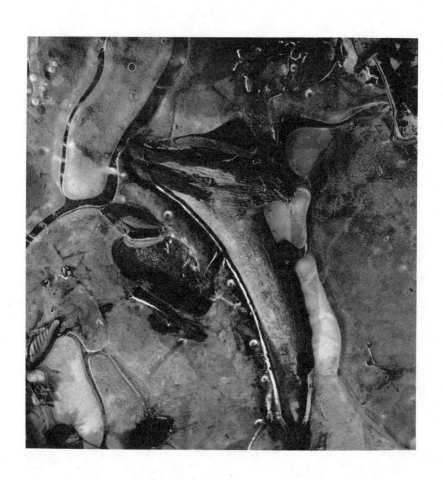

Part Two
Delusion

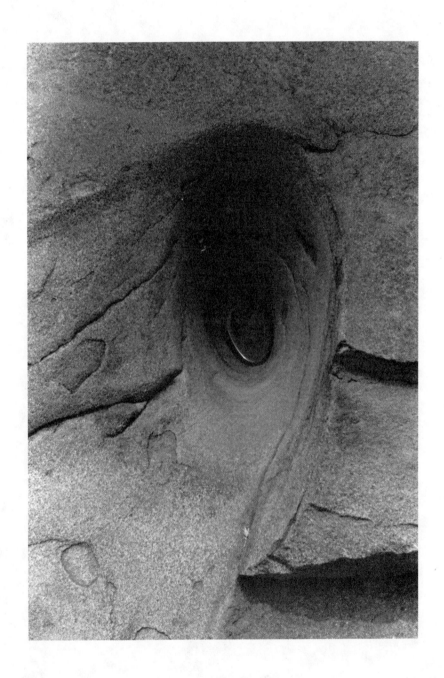

FOUR

"Yün-men's Two Sicknesses"

Case 11 of the *Book of Equanimity*

Translated by Taizan Maezumi Roshi
and Dana Fraser

Preface to the Assembly:

A bodiless person suffers illness. A handless person compounds medicine. A mouthless person takes meals. A non-receiving person has ease and comfort. Tell me, for incurable disease, what's the treatment?

Main Case:

Attention! Great Master Yün-men said, "When the light doesn't penetrate completely, there are two kinds of sicknesses. *Do you feel your mouth dry up and tongue shrivel?*[2] When wherever you are is not quite clear and there are things in front of you, that is one [sickness]. *When you see a ghost in the daylight, isn't it an illusion?* Even though you thoroughly penetrate the emptiness of all dharmas, there still somehow seems to be something. In this also, the light has not penetrated completely. *Already your chest is constricted. What does it matter if your throat is closed?*

"Again, there are two kinds of sicknesses in the Dharmakaya. *Calamities don't happen alone.* Though you reach the Dharmakaya, because Dharma-attachment is not forgotten and a view of self still persists, you plummet into the Dharmakaya side—that is one [sickness]. *Not only are there false idols outside, there's also one within.* Though you penetrate through [this], if you are negligent it's still no good. *Nursing sickness, you lose your body.* Even after a minute examination, when "What inadequacy could there be!"—this is also a sickness. *Before the doctor has gone out the door, already you're having another seizure.*

Appreciatory Verse:

> Multitudes of shapes allowed to be as is— *Let them be! How could they annoy you! If you understand them, they won't harm you.*
> Boundless, thorough liberation still obstructs the eye. *Visual rotation is attached to the tip of a sparkler.*
> To sweep out this garden, who has the strength? *Wiping traces away makes marks, trying to conceal makes more visible.*
> Concealed in one's heart, it of itself gives rise to feelings. *Doubt in the mind creates ghosts in the dark.*
> Steeped in gathering autumn lies a boat upon blue; *Submerged in stagnant water.*
> Illumined by snowy reed-flowers stands a pole with light suffused. *The still shore deceives people.*
> An old fisherman with skewered perch thinks of going to market— *Selling the merchandise, he makes a profit.*
> Carefree a leaf sails over the waves. *Finding the subtlety following the stream.*

(Editor's note: Sentences in italics above are Master Wan-sung's capping phrases for the main case and appreciatory verse. [2])

FIVE

Sitting Down in the World of Enlightenment

Commentary on "Yün-men's Two Sicknesses"

Hakuun Yasutani Roshi

Yün-men (Ummon) is Zen Master Wen-yen (Bun'en), who lived on Mt. Yün-men in Kwang-chou province. First he visited Venerable Mu-chou (Bokuju) and had an initial clarification of the great matter of life and death. Afterwards, under Zen Master Hsüeh-feng I-ts'un (Seppo Gison), he exhausted the essential mystery and became a Dharma heir of Hsüeh-feng.

Within the *Book of Equanimity* appear eight koans of Yün-men. In the *Blue Cliff Record* appear eighteen of Yün-men's koans. Yün-men undoubtedly holds a most important position with respect to Zen teaching. He is the founder of the Yün-men (Ummon) school.

Since Yün-men reveals four conditions of Zen sickness in the "Main Case," old man Wan-sung (Bansho) draws a bead on that and in his "Preface to the Assembly" sets forth four kinds of sick persons, each different from the others. Although there is a connection in that they are alike all sick and that there are gradations in the severity of their illnesses, the four persons are not the same.

"A bodiless person suffers illness. A handless person compounds medicine. A mouthless person takes meals. A non-receiving person has ease and comfort." What is this? What it says is nothing at all extraordinary. A bodiless person is one who, having dropped off mind and body, has opened his eyes. He is a person who is no longer afflicted in body and mind. The view of "things" and "self" has been totally removed. To say it in foul language, it's "peace of mind and quietness of spirit." This is no doubt an important matter, but sit down here and it becomes an illness. That is "a bodiless person suffering illness."

Being a handless person, for the first time one can freely hold things and release them. When no notice is taken of the hands being used, things can really be held or put down. The apparent increase in thinking that nowadays things are more skillfully handled is a paralyzing sickness, for sure. A person who is handless has dropped off mind and body. In addition to the whole world being the bright light of your own self and the omnipresent hue of dropped-off mind and body, heaven is heaven, earth is earth, what is manifest is the koan, you are loyal and have respect for parents—it's a world where there is no lack. Compared to the previous, this state is one stage more splendid, but sit down here and, as you might expect, it becomes an illness.

"A mouthless person takes meals." It's the same as the one before, but has greater degrees of depth and shallowness. It is a sickness one stage more acute. Take note that it is written "takes meals," not "takes medicine."[3]

What sort of person is "a non-receiving person"? In the estimation of Buddhism, it is certain that to receive is to suffer. Whether glory or status or authority or wealth, to receive any of them is suffering and the cause of suffering. And not because inheritance tax has to be paid. Common people think receiving is a pleasure; that is called "topsy-turvy pleasure." To run away, wishing not to receive anything at all, is what a Hinayana Buddhist practicer does. The Mahayana bodhisattva receives anything, but receives it without attachment. Having become an unattached person, one can for the first time appropriately and freely receive. That is real peace and comfort.

Receive everything, be unattached to everything. Unattached, you can manage everything. The ultimate of that is the non-receiving person, although he is not yet the person of great liberation. It's the place of truly great peace and comfort. However, that at once becomes the great-peace-and-comfort sickness. Become stuck even to a comfortable chair and it becomes a painful affliction. With that, four "sittings down" have been given.

"Tell me, for incurable disease what's the treatment?" An incurable disease is a difficult one that is not affected even by the powers of acupuncture and medicine. With the question of how one should medically treat the above four difficult diseases, Wan-sung comes to the "Main Case."

42   The World of Enlightenment

"Attention!" Great Master Yün-men said, "When the light doesn't penetrate completely, there are two kinds of sicknesses. When wherever you are is not quite clear and there are things in front of you, that is one."

In order to reveal four kinds of harmful influences in Zen training, Great Teacher Yün-men first separates them into two parts and says that in each part are two kinds of sicknesses.

"Light" is enlightenment. It's the bright light of your own Self. Although you may be enlightened, if it is not thoroughgoing, great enlightenment there will be a sort of faint haze: it isn't clear. That is what is called "light doesn't penetrate completely." In that, there are two kinds of sicknesses. In one of those sicknesses, there is a lack of brightness in all places, and you have no choice but to think that there are objects in front of you.

Before becoming enlightened you just think that you are here and things that are not you are over there, and you are unable to proceed even one step out of a dualistic world. Experience enlightenment, even shallow enlightenment, and you naturally understand that the thought of "objects over there" is completely mistaken—you have opened your eyes on a world where the totality is yourself. That is enlightenment.

Just to understand that oneself and others are the same is not yet enlightenment. As it says in the Ts'an t'ung ch'i (Sandokai), "To encounter the absolute is not yet enlightenment."[4] To notice the fact that all ten directions of the world are the whole body of your Self is enlightenment. When enlightenment is thorough, it is definite that outside oneself there is nothing, but if it is not thorough, then at all times and all places that face just doesn't seem to be clear. Somehow, you cannot help thinking that there seems to be something outside of yourself. This is the first sickness.

Even though you thoroughly penetrate the emptiness of all dharmas, there still somehow seems to be something. In this also, the light has not penetrated completely.

Here one more sickness is revealed. With regard to this, first keep in mind what is called "person emptied" and "dharmas emptied." "Person emptied" is only tentatively achieved. Therefore things that are not oneself seem to be seen before you. That is because the state of "dharmas emptied" has not been achieved.

When both person and dharmas are emptied, there doesn't seem to be anything remaining at all, but deeply hidden somehow, something still not empty remains like a thin haze. As if a bit of cloud remained in the vast sky, it is not yet clear. That's proof that, in truth, the bottom of the bucket is not yet broken through. If a cloud even the size of a hair remains, it expands anew, becoming a whole body of cloud. So do not be inattentive. If you are inattentive here, your dwelling in this realm immediately becomes a sickness.

> Again, there are two kinds of sicknesses in the Dharma-kaya. Though you are able to reach the Dharmakaya, because Dharma-attachment is not forgotten and a view of self still persists, you plummet into the Dharmakaya side—that is one.

Having taken care of the first of his two major divisions, Yün-men now reveals that in the next one also there are two kinds of sicknesses. The two previous kinds of sicknesses derived from the light's not having penetrated thoroughly. In the two kinds of sicknesses now to be revealed, truly the light does penetrate thoroughly. This is the stage at which "above heaven and below heaven, I alone am the revered one." The Dharmakaya is the real Self; to arrive at the Dharmakaya is to be awakened to the real Self. This is thoroughgoing, great enlightenment.

In reality, though great enlightenment is thoroughly penetrated, joy remains. Following on that is the sickness called "so many people don't know of this world that I so appreciate and revere." That is called "Dharma-attachment," attachment to the Dharma of enlightenment. The view of self discussed here is different from the ordinary view of ego: having a mental picture of enlightenment being such-and-such by gazing at it out of your own wisdom—that is called "a view of self persists." Therefore there is a plummeting into the Dharmakaya side, and a sitting down in the world of enlightenment. This is enlightenment-sickness.

> Though you penetrate through, if you are negligent it's still no good. Even after a minute examination, when "What inadequacy could there be!"—this is also a sickness.

Being able to penetrate through is thoroughgoing, great enlightenment. It is entry into the Dharmakaya world, and to discard this too is to be cured. For example, having had thoroughgoing, great enlightenment, and having discarded it and been cured, occasionally you fall into the Dharmakaya side, or a view of self arises and stays for a while without being discarded. If with might and main from moment to moment you go on paying close attention, you can't go wrong. This is called, "However you look at it there's no inadequacy." But sit down here and this too will be a sickness. With that, all four kinds of "sitting down" have been set forth. Whenever there is sitting down there is sickness, there is failure. If you don't sit down anywhere, whether your practice be profound or shallow, whether your enlightenment be bright or dim, however you happen to be you will naturally accord with the Way.

How about it? Sickness that you never thought could be so subtle has in this fashion been clearly, definitely diagnosed and plucked out. Unless you have quite a doctor you won't get treatment this complete. Great Teacher Yün-men, as you might expect, is the king of all the great doctors in the Zen world. If those people who have "one-piece enlightenment" and come to realization after realization do not fully and freely perspire over sober-minded and honest koans such as this, their realization will not be authentic.[5] It is most remarkable that *The Book of Equanimity* has delicate koans like this.

"Multitudes of shapes allowed to be as is." What are these multitudes of shapes? Don't just look over there, thinking it's the ten thousand things of heaven and earth. What is called "multitudes of shapes" is the sum total of phenomenal and noumenal manifest shapes, as well as the realms of subjective and objective insight. The Chinese characters translated "as is" mean "to have the appearance of a high mountain." What is "allowed to be"? It is to have no shortcomings. Mountains are high, rivers are long. A long thing is long Dharmakaya, a short thing is short Dharmakaya. Male is complete and female is complete. In differences, are there any insufficiencies? Or rather than insufficiencies, doesn't difference constitute their absolute value? If differences vanish, existing value also vanishes. Let's mix sweet rice cake and flavored rice in a hodgepodge and see. Wouldn't the value of both the rice cakes and the flavored rice be negated? I was impressed to hear of a follower of the Shin sect who, having experienced the compassion of Amitabha Buddha, responded, "Oh, thank you," when told that the length of the crane's leg as it is and the shortness of the duck's leg as it is are salvation itself. To see this world of no shortcomings is a leaping, first-rate awakening. But this awakening itself can at once become a sickness, as the following line indicates.

"Boundless, thorough liberation still obstructs the eye." "Boundless, thorough liberation" is the exact opposite of "multitudes of shapes." To be thoroughly liberated is for there to be neither the three times nor the ten directions.[6] It's "originally there's not one thing." No delusion, no enlightenment, no everything, no nothing. No fringe of cloud obstructing the eye. Compared with the one before, it is an enlightenment a stage more profound. However, this enlightenment at once becomes a sickness and obstructs the eye.

"To sweep out this garden, who has the strength?" To sweep the garden is to sweep out all the rubbish in one's head, to sweep out the sickness of enlightenment. This too is to be examined together with the following line.

"Concealed in one's heart, it of itself gives rise to feelings." Here "one" does not refer to someone else. It is each person, each individual. "In one's heart" is within the breast. "Gives rise to feeling" means to make mental calculations: "That principle is thus-and-so," "this principle is thus-and-so." Such mental calculations are made even if you intend not to make them—that is "concealed." That item, Dharma-attachment, is exceedingly difficult to remove. In its own time such feelings just arise. That is the sickness called "incurable disease."

"Steeped in gathering autumn lies a boat upon blue;/Illumined by snowy reed-flowers stands a pole with light suffused." Here at long last he begins to sing of a pure, refreshing state, a state of no impediments, no attachments, nothing to interfere, nothing insufficient. That is exemplified by the scenery of autumn. In autumnal countryside on a quiet river rests a boat. Both sky and water are blue. On the bank, reed-flowers glisten white as snow. The boat has been laid with its bow on the shore and just left there. It's an utterly peaceful world where nothing needs to be done. It is called "extinction manifests;" it's the realm of "great peace on earth." It is the real state of nirvana. But this too is a sickness. Stop here even a little and you will be "a dead man at the ultimate."

"An old fisherman with skewered perch thinks of going to market—/Carefree a leaf sails over the waves." The previous boat was boarded in order to save yourself, but this boat is meandering in order to save others. "Skewered perch" are sea bream speared on a skewer. "An old fisherman" is a fish-catching grandfather in whom all inclinations have been eliminated. He searches for customers with the fish he's taken, crying, "Come buy, come buy. I'm waiting for a bid. For a fair price I'll sell." Carefree, isn't he! He isn't an insistent salesman. He does not discount. To do either would destroy the Buddha Dharma. "A leaf" means a small boat. A reed bobs on the long river, going "squeak-thud, squeak-thud" as it rows along. Always, in this place or that, just right, just right, becoming one with it, carrying across donkeys, carrying across horses—that's the aspect of teaching freely. The initial line is Manjusri's wisdom. The concluding line is Avalokitesvara's compassion. United, the two become complete.

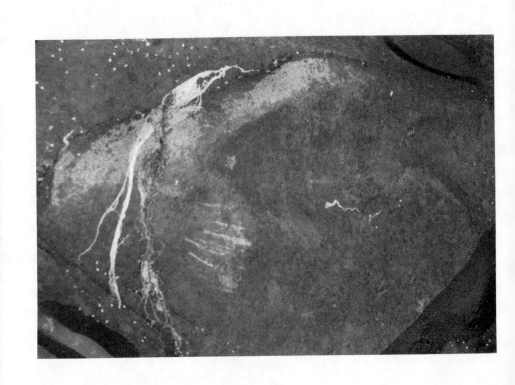

SIX

"Ghosts in the Daylight"

Commentary on the Capping Phrases

Taizan Maezumi Roshi

Yün-men mentions two kinds of sicknesses, but if we carefully examine the case we see at least five different stages, all of which come after attaining some understanding. Prior to these first stages there are still the beginning stages of practice.

The first of these sicknesses is called "the sickness of not attaining." You run around in your head, dissatisfied and uncertain, attempting to do or see something. You wonder, "What is Zen? It sounds interesting," and then you try it. Still the mind is wandering here and there. Then you come to a certain realization, and yet not being quite sure of your understanding, you tend to be attached to it. These are two kinds of initial Zen sicknesses.

This case starts with the more advanced sicknesses. For example, when you realize yourself further and you free yourself from attachment to your realization, you fall into another trap which is "the sickness of making yourself free." You see, there are all kinds of sicknesses. We are all originally Buddhas and we don't need to attempt to attain enlightenment as such. We should just sit; everything is there. In a way that's true, and yet it's a very one-sided view. We have to see both sides. One is the absolute side as expressed in the "Appreciatory Verse": "Multitudes of shapes allowed to be as is." All phenomena—mountains, rivers, trees and grasses—are as they are. Some are high, some are low; some small, some big. They are as they are, absolute. Yet being absolute, being one, there are differences.

The way in which you clearly see these two sides and see yourself in the sameness and difference, and the ways in which you share with people and all together accomplish the supreme Way, are very important. Since it's a boundless process to begin with, we can't stop anywhere. If we stick to any place, it becomes a sickness. Although Yün-men divides this into four major sicknesses, wherever there are twenty or thirty people, there are twenty or thirty different sicknesses. We need to find a way to proceed, as suggested by the koan which asks how to take a step from the top of a hundred foot pole. Wherever you are, whatever you do, that is the way to proceed.

"Attention! Great Master Yün-men said, 'When the light doesn't penetrate completely, there are two kinds of sicknesses.'" Master Wan-sung's capping phrase[2]: "Do you feel your mouth dry up and your tongue shrivel?" I feel like he is talking to me. Here Wan-sung literally refers to Yün-men and, in a way, is saying, "Hey, Master Yün-men, you attained some degree of realization. Don't you feel ashamed of yourself? Mind your own business and leave us alone." But of course by saying this, Wan-sung directly warns his disciples to realize where they stand and to know what kind of sickness they have.

"When wherever you are is not quite clear and there are things in front of you, that is one [sickness]." Wan-sung's capping phrase: "When you see a ghost in the daylight, isn't it an illusion?" To begin with, all together the world is one, and being one, what you see is all part of you. Everything appears to be yourself. If you recognize something, it is thus apart from you, like an optical illusion which doesn't exist, but which you think exists. That's a sickness. Even those who have passed the first barriers do not see this clearly. In the *Diamond Sutra* it says that our life is "like dew, like a flash of lightning," and you must really see this and contemplate it.

This reminds me of a story about the priest Ryokan, who lived a few hundred years ago in Japan, and whose poems have become quite popular in recent years. Master Ryokan practiced hard when he was young and accomplished quite well under a very famous Soto teacher. After that he lived alone in a small hut. Day after day he did nothing but play with children and talk to people and compose poems. One day he was walking on the roadside in the darkness and felt the need to defecate, so he walked into a potato field by the road and squatted. The owner of the field, who had been watching every night for potato thieves, caught Ryokan and beat him up. Another person who happened to pass by shouted at the field owner, "What are you doing? That's our priest Ryokan. Stop it." Ryokan didn't try to explain anything to the owner; he didn't even apologize. He just let the owner beat him up.

Later, Ryokan's acquaintance asked him, "Why didn't you tell him that you were the priest Ryokan?" Instead of answering, Ryokan wrote this poem:

> The one who hits and the one who is beaten,
> Both are like dew or a flash of lightning,

an allusion to the same passage from the *Diamond Sutra*.

In one way or another, the problems we get into are due to the dualism of subject and object. In themselves, subject and object are like the right hand and the left hand, man and woman, young and old, high and low, yin and yang, night and day. That's the way it is. The problem is that we become attached to one side or the other; seeing only one side, we lack understanding and can't communicate. We don't see the unity of all opposites, the whole picture. Actually the sicknesses Yün-men lists here are due to our partial, one-sided vision.

"When wherever you are is not quite clear and there are things in front of you . . . " In this first sickness we are conditioned by objects and they become our sickness. "Even though you thoroughly penetrate the emptiness of all dharmas, there still somehow seems to be something." Within yourself. You empty the dharmas, you realize that all externals are empty, are mu, and yet there is something within you which remains, called true self, emptiness, Buddha-nature. You feel it there. You are still attached to yourself and are conditioned by the subject. That's a sickness.

To penetrate the emptiness of all dharmas is not easy. Even if you see the emptiness of all things, still the light hasn't penetrated completely. Wan-sung says, "Your throat is closed." You ate something but you haven't quite swallowed it yet. These are two kinds of sicknesses in the Dharmakaya. Everything is Dharmakaya in a way.

And Wan-sung's capping phrase: "Not only are there false idols outside, there's also one within." People thought that attitudes were caused by forces outside themselves, but we are the ones who really create problems or attitudes, even after attaining enlightenment. Attaining freedom, attaining enlightenment, attaining the Dharmakaya, you make yourself free and you take initiative in life and by doing that you become arrogant. Hakuin says that he had a lot of trouble with his arrogance until he saw Shoju Rojin, who really beat him up.

"Though you penetrate through [this], if you are negligent it's still no good." Such negligence was quite common during the Sung Dynasty in China, which was the main reason that Soto practicers misunderstood koan study and the Rinzai style of practice. They saw people who, after attaining enlightenment and finishing their studies, thought that they didn't need to do zazen any more. That's a sickness indeed. Many different things have to be observed; we can't be negligent.

Wan-sung's capping phrase: "Nursing sickness, you lose your body." In order to cure your sickness, you use the medicine of enlightenment. Your sickness is cured to a certain extent but you get sicker due to the side effects. Unfortunately, this kind of thing happens even in ordinary life. It's interesting to note that our practice and our life proceed along parallel lines.

"Even after a minute examination, when 'What indadequacy could there be!'—this is also a sickness!" Wan-sung's capping phrase: "Before the doctor has gone out the door, already you're having another seizure." Do you get the point? You make yourself well, then you're relieved, but right there, something happens. What is to be the antitoxin for such a case? Our vows. Wherever we stand, in accord with our understanding, our life, we move to accomplish the four vows as followers of the Buddha Way.

Capping phrases are interesting. In koan study, students are asked to provide capping phrases from time to time to demonstrate how clear their understanding is and how well they can express themselves. Words are a most effective tool and we should know how to use them. If we use them skillfully, they have tremendous effects. For example, Master Tung-shan was once making a pilgrimage, and at a certain monastery so thoroughly defeated the head monk in Dharma combat that the head monk committed suicide out of shame. Of course I am not telling you to use words in that way, but words do have such power. In everyday life, just by using words, we quite often hurt other people and they hurt us. On the other hand, words can be used effectively to encourage people and make them happy. As part of our practice I should like us to be quite aware of what we say and how we say it.

Master T'ien-tung Hung-chih (Tendo Wanshi), who composed all of the appreciatory verses for the cases in the *Book of Equanimity*, refers to these sicknesses in the verse for this case. In the first two lines he refers to them in a rather general way: "Multitudes of shapes allowed to be as is." This includes all of us too; we are all allowed to be as is. Even the word "allowed" is, in a way, unnecessary; in fact, there is no other way to allow things to be. Everything, everybody, is just as is. If you really understand this, more than half of the practice is accomplished. But just to realize that all things are as they are is not sufficient. If you really understand it, you'll be quite content and happy, but the more clearly you see things as they are, the more you will feel that you've got to do something for other people with your understanding. This koan quite clearly indicates how we should proceed in our practice. There is another famous saying: "When the mind ceases searching, everything manifests itself right there." In other words, all sentient beings are the buddhas. But somehow we can't accept that fact, we can't be satisfied, because we separate ourselves from the very fact that we are as we are, that things are as things are. In order to make ourselves satisfied, we have to remove that division, we have to deal with our alienation.

As I always say, there are fundamentally no divisions, no conflicts, between muji, koan study and shikan-taza. Interpreting these practices superficially we can say all sorts of things, but there is not much difference between the Soto school and the Rinzai school. In a way, dividing Zen into schools is nonsense. They all must be the same thing. Realizing your true self is nothing but seeing yourself as you are. We are constantly changing; everything is changing, and we just live as long as we live, as we are.

Then we ask, what are we? What are we really? What is our unchanging essence? That's our problem. What we think we are, unfortunately, is not what we are, or at most only a very small portion of it. As I say from time to time, a large amount can't be contained in a small container. Our life is like an iceberg; we can consciously comprehend or perceive only a small portion of it. The larger portion is in the water. If we try to understand our life using our limited knowledge, understanding is impossible. What is our life? Now you know. As Buddha and all the masters tell us, it's altogether one life. Even saying "one" sounds rather silly. Since everything is nothing but your life, it's quite all right that some things are big and some are small, some are high and some are low, some are dark and some are light. But since we can't really accept things as they are, in fact, we have to practice, and the struggle starts.

The second line relates what happens after struggling: "Boundless, thorough liberation still obstructs the eye." You try hard to realize that everything is nothing but one. Those who are working on muji, work on muji and become one with muji, and eventually, sooner or later, you will realize it. The term translated here as "boundless, thorough liberation" literally means, "liberate yourself in no direction." That "no direction" becomes an obstacle. That freedom itself becomes an obstacle. If you are really free you don't talk about freedom, you don't pursue freedom. If you enjoy freedom as such, then you are not really quite free; you are still bound by freedom.

Wan-sung's capping phrase for the first line of this poem is: "Let them be. How could they annoy you? If you understand them, they won't harm you." For the second line, Wan-sung says, "Visual rotation is attached to the tip of a sparkler." When you rotate a stick which has fire on top of it, it makes a circle. Even without the fire, if you rotate the stick rapidly, it leaves a circle in the air. It's a vision, a visual rotation. The circle is perceived, but it does not exist. Now enlightenment, liberation, is like that. As long as you recognize something, you are not quite liberated yet.

The next line of the poem is: "To sweep out this garden, who has the strength?" What is this garden? The garden around your house is easy to sweep, but this garden of your mind is difficult to care for. The harder you try, the more you upset yourself. In another famous koan, Chao-chou (Joshu) was once asked by Yen-yang (Gonyo), "How about one who has nothing?" Chao-chou said, "Cast it away." Then Yen-yang said, "Having nothing, what is there to cast away?" (There he attached himself to nothing; a big trace is left.) Chao-chou said, "If so, carry it on." These koans express an advanced stage of practice, yet I think you can follow them.

"Concealed in one's heart, it of itself gives rise to feelings." Wan-sung's capping phrase: "Doubt in the mind creates ghosts in the dark." It's a rather good capping phrase. In a way, the state he's commenting on is a nice one. You are quite confident about your accomplishment and yet you are not quite clear. As it says in the "Main Case," something still remains. When your vision is not quite clear, then you start seeing all sorts of things: true self, real self, big mind, cosmic mind, absolute consciousness. They're all ghosts in the darkness.

"Steeped in gathering autumn lies a boat upon blue." This line could be a reference to the third sickness. You just sail the boat on the beautiful lake with its autumn leaves; quite nice, isn't it? However, when you are attached to it, it becomes a sickness. A beautiful autumn scene is like realizing the Dharmakaya. It's tremendously fascinating, and you think that nobody else sees it, nobody else realizes it. This is a very bad sickness. Wan-sung's capping phrase: "Submerged in stagnant water." In a way it's not at all stagnant, and yet, when you look at it from a higher standpoint, it's stagnant water. It's almost like crawling into a garbage can.

The next line, "Illumined by snowy reed-flowers stands a pole with light suffused," refers to the more accomplished state when there is nothing to say anymore. Wan-sung's capping phrase, "The still shore deceives people [in the boat]," reminds me of Dogen Zenji's beautiful statement in the *Genjokoan*: "When riding on a boat, if one watches the shore, one may assume that the shore is moving." If you stick to any place in your practice, even the most advanced accomplishment in a way becomes false. Therefore, Master T'ien-tung expresses in the final two lines how we should proceed in our practice: "An old fisherman with skewered perch thinks of going to market./Carefree a leaf sails over the waves." It's interesting to appreciate who the old fisherman is, and what the perch is. There are all kinds of sicknesses, all kinds of lives. Even masters like Yün-men and Bodhidharma skewered them all together on one stick and tried to sell them. To whom? To those who really wanted them.

"Carefree a leaf sails over the waves." Carefree: totally free, without restriction, without urging, proceeding in accord with the environment, the circumstances and the time in which one lives. Just go with it like a small leaf flowing along with the stream. Wan-sung's capping phrase for the old fisherman is, "Selling the merchandise, he makes a profit." What kind of merchandise? This profit is a priceless profit. This reminds me of the last stage of the ten oxherding pictures and also of another famous poem in which an idiot sage is hired to fill up a well with snow. In order to do that sort of work, you have to be carefree; you can't expect anything. As each pile of snow is dumped into the deep well, it immediately melts. But it doesn't matter, we just do it.

"Carefree a leaf sails over the waves." And Wan-sung's capping phrase: "Finding the subtlety following the stream." I leave that line to you. It's a hard koan but a nice one. I hope all of you will accomplish that far, and enjoy life together.

The Hazy Moon of Enlightenment   55

SEVEN

What Are Our Delusions?: Dharma Dialogue

with Tetsugen Glassman Sensei

When he achieved enlightenment, Shakyamuni Buddha said, "How wonderful, how wonderful! How truly miraculous! All sentient beings have the wisdom and virtue of the Tathagata." That is, everything, just as it is, is fully enlightened. We just can't see it, just can't accept it. And why not? Because we're deluded. And what are these delusions? How can it be that at the very same time that we are completely enlightened, that we are the Buddha, we are also deluded? In this room there are thirty or forty people, and there are at least thirty or forty different types of delusions, and thirty or forty Buddhas.

In the koan "Yün-men's Two Sicknesses," the eleventh case of *The Book of Equanimity*, Master Yün-men talks about two major types of delusion that we have when we have not yet completely realized what enlightenment is, what Buddha is, what the Dharmakaya is. He then talks about two major categories of sickness or delusion we have after completely realizing what enlightenment is, what the Dharmakaya is, what Buddha is.

His first major category is when, although we have glimpsed our true nature, still we perceive things as separate from ourselves. The world's nothing but one thing, yet how many of us can see it that way? If you perceive anything as being separate from yourself, you fall into this first deluded state. For example, when we work on the koan muji, we put ourselves fully into this *muuuuu!* A car goes by and the car bothers us. Right there we perceive something separate. We keep working, and finally we reach the point where there is nothing outside of mu. The only thing that exists is this mu!

Master Lin-chi (Rinzai) talks about it in the same way. First we empty the subject: the I disappears and only the object, only mu exists. Having done that, the second category takes over and we glimpse our true nature, we see that everything is nothing but ourselves. Yet still we recognize something internally, still we think of ourselves as ourselves; subject is still there. That's the second major deluded state: I exist.

Then Master Lin-chi talks about emptying both the subjective and objective worlds; neither subject nor object exists. That's the state when we're truly working on muji. Then we polish up, clarify, and work for years to fully realize and actualize what this enlightened state is, what our true self is, what Buddha is. Along the way we fall into Yün-men's next stage: having completely seen this world of oneness, the Dharmakaya, having fully realized what enlightenment is, what Buddha is, still somehow we have some trace of self, and with that comes conceit and arrogance. "He doesn't know what he's talking about. *I* know." We still can't realize that it's all one thing, that it's nonsense to think that we know more than anyone else.

Then we polish up our practice further. Having realized our true self and come to the point where we think we've accomplished enough, the path seems to end. But it's a giant trap. This is the fourth stage that Yün-men talks about. There is no end, no matter how much we realize, no matter how deep our understanding is. Mountains and mountains above that. These are Yün-men's four major categories.

Now I say that each one of us is nothing but the Buddha. Each one of us is completely enlightened. That being the case, what are our delusions? Please come up and let's talk about it.

Q: A lot of times I recognize obstructions. How to deal with those obstructions? To fight them seems like rattling the bars of a cage, "Let me out, let me out," and as we become stronger, the obstructions become stronger too. Yet to accept them and just sit doesn't seem right either. So what do we do?
Sensei: What are your obstructions?
Q: Hard to put a finger on them.

Sensei: If you can't put a finger on them, they can't be obstructions.
Q: But they come up and I recognize them as obstructions.
Sensei: Name your obstructions.
Q: Fear, separation.
Sensei: Those aren't obstructions. Those are virtues.
Q: How so?
Sensei: How so? There are always two ways of looking at things. You can look at a blade of grass and say, "It can't fly. It's limited." Or you can look at a blade of grass and say, "It's green. Green is its virtue." We can look at a tiger and say, "It's dangerous; it kills other animals." That's an obstruction. Or we can say, "It's powerful; it's an excellent hunter." That's a virtue. How so?

Q: Since I have the wisdom and virtue of the Tathagata, my greatest delusion must then be that I should continue to do zazen, that I should continue to scrub delusion clean.
Sensei: The first thing I thought of when you said that was, Is it a delusion to eat? Is it a delusion to get up in the morning? Is it a delusion to shower? Is it a delusion to read books?
Q: That's what I did before I came here.
Sensei: You did zazen before you came here. You did zazen before you were born. And on top of all of this, we have to act out our delusions because we are deluded, and that very delusion is enlightenment.
Q: We vow to "put an end to delusions."
Sensei: Please make your vows every night. Those very vows are nothing but our greatest delusion, and without those vows this would not be Mahayana Buddhism.

Q: Having heard you speak, a very big, strong man comes into the zendo smoking a cigarette and says, "Yeah, I'm the Buddha." And he walks up to the altar and he drops his ashes on Manjusri and continues smoking, and when he's told to stop he just laughs. When we try to throw him out he beats us with a stick. He is very strong and we can't put him out, he just says, "Ha, yes, I'm the Buddha! What could be wrong?" How would you treat that man?
Sensei: Would you please get up and remove the cat (*pointing to a cat that has managed to slip into the zendo*). There's a cat in the zendo.
Q: (*Gets up and carries out the cat amidst great laughter.*)
Sensei: Thank you for your answer.

Q: It's only natural that I hope that Yün-men's illnesses are somehow contagious.

Sensei: They are. Have no fear. Yün-men's sicknesses are contagious.

Q: I'm very grateful to be in the hospital.

Q: It's pretty clear that everything is ourself, and yet there is this delusion that somehow it isn't quite right. Delusion keeps creeping in; it's like an old friend, you know. We can invite it in and treat it like a member of the family also, but somehow it's pretty uncomfortable and pretty unpleasant to have around. It feels more like a burden or like that loud man with the cigarette. Who is the one who is able to make this delusion feel at home?

Sensei: It's interesting. Yün-men talks about these delusions as sicknesses, but we could also talk about them in a positive way. This is our path of training. We have to see each of these steps, and in so doing, all of these questions that we come up with just drop away one by one. We practice, do zazen, develop our concentration, our awareness, sit until all of the externals drop away; that's our first stage. Then who can come into the zendo? We have to see that and then the question resolves itself. Then we sit, we practice, and the subject drops away; and then our obstructions, where are they? Our lack of confidence, whose lack of confidence? Our frustrations, whose frustrations? Let that subject drop away, and how can these questions not be resolved?

Q: Seems like there's a split-second in every moment of zazen (snaps his fingers) when subject/object arises. Suddenly something appears and you grab it and you know, "that's me." And there are times when that just never appears.

Sensei: I'm not talking about split-seconds.

Q: What are you talking about?

Sensei: I'm talking about our life. Just practice. Please keep practicing and we will see that those split-seconds you're talking about and our life that I'm talking about are the same thing.

Q: Is it all right to think that somebody knows more than we do?

Sensei: Does anybody know more than you do?

Q: I really would like to learn something now.

Sensei: There is only one way to do that and that's to fully empty your cup. I remember the first time Koryu Roshi came here, I believe it was during his first sesshin. He talked about how wonderful it was to wake up in the morning and have Bodhidharma there talking to him—those crickets. As we empty our cup, what else could be teaching us? Who else knows more? But with our cup full, Shakyamuni Buddha standing next to us doesn't make any sense.

Q: Bodhidharma came and talked with Koryu Roshi in the mornings?

Sensei: Yep.

Q: Mama cat comes and sleeps with me sometimes. Thank you for your answer.

Q: Last weekend at the seminar we were talking of Tung-shan's *five positions*, and you said something about the fifth one being delusion within delusion. What's the difference between our delusions and those delusions within delusions?

Sensei: For the record we could fix it later, but you're mixing up references. "Delusions within delusions" is from the *Genjokoan* by Dogen Zenji. "Delusions within delusions" means making those vows that we make each night, but making them with the utmost confidence that there are no sentient beings, with the utmost confidence that there are no desires, with the utmost confidence that there are no dharmas, and with the utmost confidence that there is no Buddha Way.* Knowing that and taking these vows, that's delusion within delusion.

Q: Thank you for your answer.

Q: I'd like to know a generalized definition of "delusion."

Sensei: A generalized definition of delusion. You sound like a mathematician. Give me a specific definition. Mathematicians generalize from specifics.

Q: You mean an example of a delusion?

Sensei: Sure.

Q: OK, being separate from another person.

Sensei: So a generalization of that is, "You are separate from everything else."

Q: OK. What I'm wondering is exactly what you mean by delusion. When we talk so much about enlightenment being delusion, and delusion being enlightenment, it's . . .

Sensei: What is enlightenment?

Q: I would think that it is just seeing things as they are, and delusion is not seeing things as they are. But you know, of course, if enlightenment is delusion, and delusion is enlightenment, it doesn't quite come out. (*Laughter*)

Sensei: One way of answering that question very easily is, if enlightenment is seeing things as they are, and delusion is the opposite, then it's seeing things as they are not. Can you see things as they are not?

Q: I feel myself as separate from things.

Sensei: Do you see this stick?

Q: Yes.

Sensei: This is the very thing. Delusion is not accepting that you're seeing things as they are. But you can't see them differently.

Q: Thank you for your answer.

Q: I feel as if my biggest delusion is that I am deluded, and sometimes I feel very, very deluded. What do I do about it?

Sensei: That's why we have to practice. The title of Kennett Roshi's book, *Selling Water by the River*, is a line from Dogen Zenji's writings. It's amazing, but everybody wants to buy it, and we have no choice but to sell it and to wait in line to buy it. Delusions are crazy and so we practice, and that's enlightenment. Let's appreciate that craziness.

Q: How do you empty a bottomless cup?

Sensei: Our first step really is not to break away the bottom of the cup, but to empty it and let something fall into it. Then, after doing that, empty it again and let something fall into it, then again empty it and let something fall into it. It's important when we empty it to really empty that cup, which means to wipe it so clean that there's nothing that interferes with the next thing coming into it. If we do this often enough, eventually the cup breaks and becomes bottomless and sideless and there is no more cup. But first let's start off with the easy vow and try to empty it and listen and accept what we hear, and empty it and listen and accept, and empty it and listen and accept.

Dogen Zenji puts it another way. We have to make vows. Then making vows, raising our aspirations, we practice. And practicing, we realize something. Then we have to get rid of that, and again we have to make our vows. That's cleaning our cup. Then practice so that we can accept it, and then realize. In this way our practice just goes on and on.

Q: What if you never get down to cleaning it, if it's always full no matter how much you pour out?
Sensei: Start at the beginning; make your vows.
Q: Thank you.

Q: When we come across situations where we have to do something that we don't like to do, can we help our practice by purposely putting ourselves into that situation?
Sensei: Sounds scary to me. I don't think I've ever done that. If you find yourself in the situation of having to do something you don't really want to do, look at why you're in such a situation. Sometimes we kid ourselves and say, "Why do I do this zazen? I don't really want to do it." But if we really didn't want to be here doing it, we wouldn't be here. But sometimes, we really don't want to do something and then to force ourselves into it seems wrong to me. But just see why you have to do it, then do what you have to do. Nobody's here by accident.

Q: I hope I'm always standing in line waiting to buy the water; I know I will be.
Sensei: Naw, someday you'll start selling it. (*Laughter*)
Q: Who am I going to sell it to?
Sensei: There'll be people; don't worry.
Q: What's the difference between buying and selling it?
Sensei: That's a good question. What's the difference?
Q: Financially speaking, the person who is . . . (*Laughter*)
Sensei: (*Smiling*) That's enough!

Enlightenment and delusion. As you know, Dogen Zenji wrote that enlightenment is delusion, delusion is enlightenment. He was a brilliant monk, and practiced vigorously and earnestly. In fact, he had already completed koan study in Japan before going to China where he practiced at some of the strictest monasteries. Although in his later years he writes that "enlightenment is delusion," in his earlier years he was constantly questioning, "Maybe that's so, but why don't I realize it? Why did all those Patriarchs and masters practice so hard?" To resolve that question, he practiced diligently for a long time. Some of us will practice the way he did, most of us won't. No matter how we practice, the fact will remain, enlightenment is delusion, delusion is enlightenment.

Father Kennedy, a Jesuit priest, was telling me the other night that in Kamakura there is a group of Jesuits sitting with Yamada Roshi, and that one of them, a German priest, often calls out on the way to the zendo, "Tonight we sit until kensho, right?" If we have such strong determination, there is a one hundred percent guarantee that we'll resolve the matter of enlightenment and delusion. To see our true self is a wonderful first step. Let's keep buying and selling that water together.

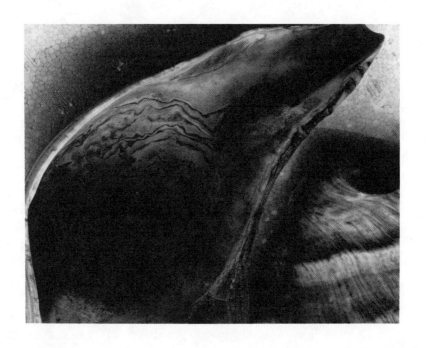

Part Three

Enlightenment
In Action

EIGHT

"The Eight Awarenesses of the Enlightened Person"

Dogen Zenji's *Hachidainingaku*
Translated by Taizan Maezumi Roshi
and Francis Dojun Cook

All Buddhas are enlightened persons. Those things which the enlightened persons are aware of are called the "eight awarenesses of the enlightened person." To become aware of this Dharma is the cause for nirvana. Our master, Shakyamuni Buddha, taught this [Dharma] on the last night before entering *parinirvana*.

First: *Having few desires:*

> Not seeking too much among the objects of the
> five desires which are not yet obtained is called
> "having few desires."

The Buddha says: "You monks should know that because those who have many desires search for fame and profit, there is much suffering. Those who have few desires look around less and desire little; therefore, they have no worry of this sort. You should practice if only to have few desires. Needless to say, having few desires produces many merits.

"Those who have few desires do not have to flatter in order to ingratiate themselves with others. Also, they withstand temptations from the various sense organs. One who practices 'having few desires' has neither worry nor fear, for his mind is peaceful. Whatever he comes into contact with, he finds that it is enough, and he never lacks anything. Having few desires, he is in nirvana. This is called 'having few desires.' "

Second: *Knowing how to be satisfied:*

> Knowing how much to take of those things
> which one already has is called "knowing
> how to be satisfied."

The Buddha says: "You monks should contemplate knowing how to be satisfied if you wish to be liberated from suffering. The dharma of knowing how to be satisfied is the realm of riches, comfort, peace and tranquility. Those who know how to be satisfied are happy and comfortable even when sleeping on the ground. Those who do not know how to be satisfied are not satisfied even when dwelling in a heavenly palace. Those who do not know how to be satisfied are poor even though they are wealthy, while those who know how to be satisfied are wealthy even though they have little. Those who do not know how to be satisfied and are always tempted by the five desires are consoled by those who know how to be satisfied. This is called 'knowing how to be satisfied.' "

Third: *Enjoying serenity and tranquility:*

> Being apart from all disturbances and dwell-
> ing alone in a quiet place is called "enjoying
> serenity and tranquility."

The Buddha says: "If you monks seek joy and peace in the serenity and tranquility of non-doing, you should keep away from disturbances and dwell alone in a quiet place. Those who dwell in quiet places are praised and respected both by Sakrendra, chief of the gods, and by celestial beings. Therefore, casting away attachment to yourself and others, dwell alone in a quiet place and contemplate the cause of suffering. Those who desire the company of other people suffer from their relationship with them, just as a tree will be broken and die when many birds roost in it. The bondage of worldly involvement will drown you in suffering, just as an old elephant drowns in the mud because he is unable to get out by himself. To liberate oneself from complicated involvements is called 'detachment.' "

Fourth: *Exerting meticulous effort:*

> Exerting oneself meticulously and unceas-
> ingly in various beneficial practices is called
> "meticulous effort." Be precise, not careless;
> proceed forward, do not regress.

The Buddha says: "If you monks exert meticulous effort, nothing
will be difficult to accomplish. Therefore, you should make an effort
to practice carefully, for when water flows constantly against a big
rock, even a small amount of water will eventually dig out a large
hole. But if one who practices becomes lax, it will be impossible to
accomplish anything. It is like trying to start a fire by rubbing two
sticks together; if you stop rubbing before the wood gets hot, you
can't start a fire. This is what is meant by 'meticulous effort.' "

Fifth: *Not forgetting [right] thought:*

> This is also called "maintaining right thought."
> "Protecting the Dharma and not losing it"
> means "right thought," or "not forgetting
> [right] thought."

The Buddha says: "If you monks seek both a good teacher and
good protection and support, nothing is better than 'not forgetting
[right] thought.' For those who do not forget [right] thought, the robber-
like multitude of deluding passions cannot break in. For this reason,
you should always keep right thought in your mind and regulate it
well, for if you lose this thought, all sorts of merits and virtues will
also be lost. If the power of this thought is strong and firm, then even
though you mingle with the robber-like five desires, you will not be
injured, just as, if you go into battle dressed in armor, you will not
fear the enemy. This is the meaning of 'not forgetting [right] thought.' "

Sixth: *Practicing samadhi:*

> Dwelling in the Dharma undisturbed is what
> is called "samadhi."

The Buddha says: "When you monks unify your minds, the mind
is in samadhi. Since the mind is in samadhi, you know the charac-

teristics of the creation and destruction of the various phenomena in the world. For this reason, you should constantly practice with diligence and cultivate all kinds of samadhi. When you gain samadhi, the mind is not scattered, just as those who protect themselves from floods guard the levy. This is also true for practice. For the sake of the "water of wisdom," then, cultivate samadhi well, and do not let it leak out. This is called 'samadhi.' "

Seventh: *Cultivating wisdom:*

> Wisdom is aroused by hearing, reflecting,
> practicing, and realizing.

The Buddha says: "When you monks have wisdom, you are without greed. Always reflect upon yourselves; do not lose this wisdom. In this way you can thus attain liberation in my Dharma. One who does not is neither a follower of the Way (monk) nor a white-robe (layman), nor is there any other name for him. True wisdom is a stout boat which crosses the sea of old age, sickness and death; it is also a great bright torch in pitch black ignorance; a good medicine for all sick people; a sharp axe which fells the tree of delusion. Therefore, by means of this wisdom which is heard, reflected upon, and practiced, you will increase your merit. When one has the illumination of wisdom, even though one's eyes are merely physical eyes, one is a 'clear-seeing person.' This is what is meant by 'wisdom.' "

Eighth: *Avoiding idle talk:*

> Having realization and being free from dis-
> crimination is what is called "avoiding idle
> talk." To totally know the true form of all
> things is the same as being without idle talk.

The Buddha says: "When you monks engage in various kinds of idle talk, your minds are disturbed. Although you have left home [and become monks], you are still not liberated. Therefore, you monks must quickly abandon mind-disturbing idle talk. If you would like to attain the joy of the extinction of delusion, you must first simply extinguish the affliction of idle talk. This is what 'avoiding idle talk' means."

These are the eight awarenesses of a Buddha. Within each one all eight are contained, thus making a total of sixty-four. Broadly speaking, the number could be infinite, but for the sake of simplicity, sixty-four are enough. This is the final teaching of the great master, the revered Shakyamuni, and it is the ultimate teaching of the Mahayana, spoken at midnight on February fifteenth. He then entered complete nirvana without any further Dharma teaching.

The Buddha said: "You monks should continually and single-mindedly strive to accomplish the Way. Every dharma in the world, whether active or non-active, is characterized by destructibility and unrest. Now please keep quiet and say no more. Time passes on, and I shall enter complete nirvana. This is my final admonition."

For this reason, disciples of the Tathagata learn and practice these eight awarenesses without fail. One who neither knows nor studies nor practices these is not a disciple of the Buddha, for these are the Tathagata's *shobogenzo nehan myoshin* ("treasury of the true Dharma eye, marvellous mind of nirvana"). In spite of this, there are many nowadays who do not know it, and those who have seen it or heard of it are few; their ignorance of it is due to their being caught up by demons' temptations, and those who did not cultivate enough good roots in previous existences have neither seen it nor heard of it. In the old days, in the periods of the "true Dharma" and the "imitative Dharma," the Buddha's disciples all knew, studied, and penetrated it. Nowadays, hardly one or two among a thousand monks knows the eight awarenesses of the Buddha. How pitiful it is! There is nothing to compare with the barbarians of this decadent time.

However, today the Tathagata's true Dharma is spread over the universe, and the pure Dharma has not yet been extinguished. You must quickly begin to practice it. Don't be sluggish and lazy! It is difficult to encounter the Buddha-Dharma even after countless eons, and it is also difficult to acquire a human form. Even if you acquire a human body, it is better to be a human being in the three territories, and even better to have a human form in the southern territory because there one can see the Buddha, hear the Dharma, make one's home-departure, and attain the Way. Those who died before the Tathagata entered final nirvana neither learned nor practiced these eight awarenesses of the Buddha. Now we see, hear, learn and practice them through the power of having cultivated good roots in previous existences. Now, to practice them and increase them in successive lives, to attain peerless enlightenment without fail, and to expound them for the sake of all sentient beings, is to be the same as Shakyamuni Buddha, without any difference.

The "Eight Awarenesses of a Buddha" of the *Shobogenzo* was written at Eihei-ji on January sixth, 1253. Now, in the year 1255 on the day before the training session ends, Gien has been ordered to make this copy and proofread it. The foregoing essay was written by our late teacher during his last illness. When I reflect upon the fact that the Japanese version of *Shobogenzo* was to be newly rewritten to make one hundred volumes, this becomes the twelfth volume [after the first seventy-five volumes]. After his illness, he gradually got worse and worse, so that he had to give up his writing. Therefore, this volume is the very last instruction of our late teacher, and unfortunately, we will not be able to see the intended one hundred chapters. It is most regrettable. Those who love and revere our former teacher should copy and preserve this. This is the final teaching of our late master. (Ejo recorded this.)

NINE

Introduction to the Eight Awarenesses

Now that we've discussed enlightenment and the various kinds of delusion that cloud enlightenment, let's go on to consider these eight awarenesses, which are one way of looking at the actualization of enlightenment in everyday life.

According to the *Mahaparinirvana Sutra*, the eight awarenesses were the final teaching of Shakyamuni Buddha before his death. Interestingly enough, "The Eight Awarenesses of the Enlightened Person" (*Hachidainingaku*), the chapter translated here from Dogen Zenji's *Shobogenzo* (Treasury of the True Dharma Eye), was the last chapter of the *Shobogenzo* written by Dogen Zenji before his own death in 1253. By the time this chapter was written, Dogen Zenji had attracted a large following of monks at Eiheiji, the monastery built for him in Echizen province by a lay disciple. However, his health had been failing for several years, and we can imagine that he was aware of his impending death and chose these eight awarenesses, these very basic aspects of our practice, as the subject of one of his last teishos in order to encourage his disciples.

In many ways, the eight awarenesses resemble various other categories and lists that appear in early Indian sutras and are attributed to the Buddha, for example, the eightfold path, the ten grave precepts and the six paramitas. In fact, more or less direct parallels can be drawn between such lists: the awareness of wisdom can be directly paralleled to "right understanding," which is the first step of the eightfold path; the eighth awareness, "avoiding idle talk," parallels "right speech;" "exerting meticulous effort" corresponds to "right effort;" "samadhi" to "right samadhi;" and so on. Similar parallels might also be drawn with the ten precepts and the six paramitas, but it's not necessary for us to explore them here. Many of those lists were teachings of the Buddha presented rather casually to his disciples and later recorded and standardized. Consequently, many of the apparent correspondences were actually overlaps or repetitions, because Buddha would often repeat himself by saying very much the same thing in different words.

The eight awarenesses also resemble the eightfold path in that we can look at either of them not as a linear progression or as a list of unrelated qualities, but as a circular or spiral development which can begin at any point, each stage in turn encouraging the development of the next. For example, if we have few desires, then of course we'll find it easier to know how to be satisfied. And knowing how to be satisfied, we don't have to seek serenity, but very naturally we will rejoice in the serenity and peacefulness of body and mind that arises from knowing how to be satisfied. Then having serenity, meticulous effort will arise naturally in the course of our practice, and having this right, meticulous effort, we can know what it is not to forget right thought. This constant mindfulness and remembrance of who we are, of ourselves as the Three Treasures (Buddha, Dharma and Sangha), then encourages the growth of samadhi. And of course, samadhi turns into wisdom. Interestingly enough, the eight awarenesses do not end with wisdom or samadhi, as do similar lists, but with "avoiding idle talk." If we realize that everything is in its very nature empty, then there will be no problem, our talk will not be idle talk. Then having this wisdom and avoiding idle talk, we won't stir up desires unnecessarily—and the circle begins again.

In fact, this circle closely resembles the spiral of practice described by Dogen Zenji, which begins with raising the bodhi-mind. Raising the bodhi-mind relates to having few desires, knowing how to be satisfied and enjoying serenity, that is, clearing the path and raising the desire and the aspiration to practice. Then we practice, exerting meticulous effort and not forgetting who we are. Then we attain realization, which corresponds to right samadhi, right wisdom and avoiding idle talk in its deepest sense. After realization we finally attain nirvana and then start again by throwing it away and raising the bodhi-mind, practicing and realizing. In both cases the meaning is fundamentally the same: practice endlessly advances, each stage gives rise to and enriches the next, and we must beware of getting stuck at any one point along the way.

On one level, then, the eight awarenesses are a description of how our practice actually proceeds. But more fundamentally, how should we relate to the eight awarenesses? Are they moral or ethical guidelines, or are they actually aspects of the enlightened nature or a description of the Buddha himself? As the title suggests, these eight awarenesses are in fact the awarenesses of the Buddha, ways of describing the Buddha himself. But again, who is the Buddha? We ourselves are the Buddha, and these are ways of talking about our life and our practice.

One convenient way of looking at the eight awarenesses is by using three modes commonly used to interpret the precepts: Hinayana, Mahayana, and Buddha-nature. According to the Hinayana mode, the precepts are very strictly interpreted; if we do anything that the precepts prohibit, we're violating those precepts. The Mahayana mode is much more flexible and appropriate to particular circumstances. Depending on the time, the place, the person and the extent or the amount, the precepts are interpreted differently. For example, take "do not tell a lie." There are many famous stories in Buddhism about the truth being told inappropriately and doing harm to others. At times, what seems like a lie is actually the most appropriate thing to say, according to the time, the place, the person and the amount. The third way of interpreting the precepts, Buddha-nature, says that there is fundamentally no separation between ourselves and others, and that if we are really aware of this no-separation and really act in accord with it, then it's impossible to violate the precepts from the very beginning. All being intrinsically one, there can be no violation of the precepts.

In the same way, the eight awarenesses can be looked at from these three points of view. In one sense, these eight awarenesses are strict guidelines for our practice. That is, we should learn how to be satisfied, we should learn to enjoy serenity, we should develop right effort and we should not forget that we are the Three Treasures. From the Mahayana point of view, yes, we should have few desires, but there are times when certain desires are appropriate. Knowing how to be satisfied, enjoying serenity—we can't strictly interpret this serenity. There are times when we have to be in the midst of activity and commotion for the sake of being with other people and helping them in their practice. The same can be said of the other eight awarenesses.

As for the Buddha-nature way of interpreting them, they are indeed the eight awarenesses of the enlightened person. The Buddha, finding no separation between himself and other beings, very naturally acts in this way. Feeling no separation from others, Buddha naturally has few desires. Feeling no separation from others, from our surroundings, from what is happening right now, of course we can't help but be satisfied, enjoying the serenity of things as they are. When we know the oneness of ourselves and others, effort becomes right effort, our activity becomes the embodiment of wisdom, and no talk is idle talk.

With this in mind, let's go on and study each of the eight awarenesses, keeping in mind that they're not talking about some distant goal or the life of someone who lived many hundreds of years ago, but are actually talking about our life right now. Buddha addresses himself to "you monks," but he is talking to all of us.

(Editor's note: In the chapters that follow, commentary is by Taizan Maezumi Roshi, and discussion is led by Tetsugen Glassman Sensei.)

TEN

"Having Few Desires"

All Buddhas are enlightened persons. Those things which the enlightened persons are aware of are called the "eight awarenesses of the enlightened person." To become aware of this Dharma is the cause for nirvana. Our master, Shakyamuni Buddha, taught this [Dharma] on the last night before entering *parinirvana*.

First: *Having few desires:*

> Not seeking too much among the objects of the
> five desires which are not yet obtained is called
> "having few desires."

The Buddha says: "You monks should know that because those who have many desires search for fame and profit, there is much suffering. Those who have few desires look around less and desire little; therefore they have no worry of this sort. You should practice if only to have few desires. Needless to say, having few desires produces many merits.

"Those who have few desires do not have to flatter in order to ingratiate themselves with others. Also, they withstand temptations from the various sense organs. One who practices 'having few desires' has neither worry nor fear, for his mind is peaceful. Whatever he comes into contact with, he finds that it is enough, and he never lacks anything. Having few desires, he is in nirvana. This is called 'having few desires.' "

Commentary

If we carefully examine ourselves we see all kinds of desires, and yet actually, there is nothing to gain. At the same time there is nothing to lose either. That's the very plain state of existence, that's our life. In other words, it's always fulfilled in just the right way. We have it, we are using it, we have enough. Having less desire is, in its best sense, to realize this fact. Yet somehow we don't think we have enough. We think that something is lacking, and so we have all kinds of desires. These "five desires" that Dogen Zenji mentions are just five major examples.

If we really see the truth of the five desires which are not yet gained, then we see *prajna* wisdom. And having prajna wisdom, seeing that there is nothing outside of ourselves, we naturally desire little. When we read this, it's not at all difficult to appreciate with our common sense. The less we have, the fewer problems we have. In our life, we hear people complain that they earn lots of money, and yet all the money disappears. Why? They have more bills to pay, they buy all kinds of gadgets for pleasure. The more they have, the more headaches they have, too. A friend who works at the bank tells me quite often, "These people who have lots of money are so unhappy. It's painful to watch them." The more they have, the more trouble they have. It is so true that if you have less, you don't need to worry. It's very easy to understand, isn't it?

Of course, there is also the desire to practice, the desire to accomplish the Way. We might call this kind of desire "right desire," because it arises out of a wish or an aspiration to benefit other people before thinking about ourselves. But usually when we speak about desire we mean the five major ones: desire for money, for wealth; desire for material things, which in a narrower sense is a desire for the opposite sex, but in a broader sense is a desire for anything which has form; desire for food; desire for fame; and desire for sleep.

Another interesting way to understand these desires is to correlate them with our senses: desires of eye, ear, nose, tongue, body and consciousness. To say that they "want" may seem rather peculiar, but actually our senses create certain desires, being attracted by sounds, smells, sights, tastes, thoughts, and touchable objects. What creates the real difficulty, though, is our ignorance. And why? We are ignorant simply because we don't have right wisdom. What veils right wisdom? Delusions.

There are many delusions, but theoretically we say there are six basic kinds of delusion. The first one is greed. The five desires come under this greed. Being greedy, we want all kinds of things. The second one which hinders our wisdom is anger. Having strong like or dislike for something, we can't see it clearly. The third one is ignorance or folly. In Japanese we say, *mu myo*, literally "no light," "darkness." Since it's dark, you don't know where you are or what you have to do.

The fourth one is conceit. There are all kinds of conceit; for example, when you pretend to underestimate yourself, that too is conceit. Of course, the most common one is for you to think you are the best in the world, which is true conceit.

The next one is doubt. In this case, it is doubt about the Three Treasures, doubt about yourself, doubt about causation. The sixth one is called "wrong views." There are all kinds of wrong views that prevent us from having wisdom. The last two among the delusions just enumerated, doubt and wrong views, are actually the ones that are supposed to be taken care of by having kensho. If your experience is clear enough, you will have a very good understanding, and will no longer doubt.

In actual practice, delusions like greed, anger, ignorance, conceit, doubt, and wrong views are not only habitual, but exist in the emotional domain as well, and so are difficult to take care of. As with the five desires, it takes a long time to tame them. We will see in a later chapter how to have right effort and how to pursue our practice. By our practice, by our effort, by our wisdom, we can take care of these delusions and desires little by little.

Discussion

Q: Telling someone to have few desires sounds straightforward enough, but I find it difficult to accomplish.
Sensei: The first thing I'd like to mention, which is true of all eight awarenesses, is their simplicity. Many things in Zen seem very esoteric or hard to grasp. There are either no words to express them, or the words we use are foreign to our normal verbal sphere. These eight awarenesses can usually be experienced easily. The words are

simple. Interestingly, both Buddha's and Dogen Zenji's last talks are their simplest. They talk about such obvious things as what to do about desires, how to be satisfied, and how to enjoy serenity and tranquility. But in a way that's the key. Just realizing and actually practicing these simple things is all that Zen is about. The problem is that it is hard to be so simple. It's hard to really make these things part of us, and so the practice becomes difficult. But once you've accomplished that practice, the things we're talking about become very simple.

Q: I desire to be better than I am.
Sensei: Whatever you have, that's what you have. Then you may say, "Well, why aren't I such and such?" Because you're not such and such; that's having a desire for things that you don't already have, for things not already obtained. Grass really intrigues me. Grass is green, and for grass to have a desire to be purple, or for us to have a desire for grass to be purple, doesn't make sense. Grass is green. Certainly we can desire it to be purple, but that's meaningless and just creates conflict. If we eliminate all those kinds of desires, that is, desires for things which are not, things we are not, then right there is nirvana. But it's not an easy thing to do, and it's not a passing thing. It's the place where we are. Living in the realm of who and what we are, we can accomplish continually, practice continually. There is so much we can do. But as soon as we start reaching out for things that are not us, we run into problems, and it's obvious that we run into problems because they're not us. It's just like wanting grass to be purple. You can fight your whole life for that, but it's absurd.

Q: If nirvana is accepting myself just as I am, what is kensho?
Sensei: I want to differentiate between the first breakthrough, or first opening, and kensho. Deluded views and doubt are eliminated by what we call kensho, the enlightened state. Kensho is seeing true nature. It's called the great enlightenment experience, and is accompanied by the elimination of deluded views and of all doubt that you are the Three Treasures, that you are enlightened, that you are the Buddha. The first four delusions—greed, anger, ignorance, and conceit—are still there.

   This enlightenment experience culminates the first part of Zen training, "catching the bull" in the ten oxherding pictures. Then we've got to tame it, and that takes twenty, thirty, forty years or more, depending on how ingrained and conditioned our body and our memory is. It's a lifetime practice. People usually want somebody they think is well accomplished in Zen training to be perfect, to have no more greed, no more anger, no more ignorance, no more conceit. It doesn't work that way. It's a lifetime process.

ELEVEN

"Knowing How to Be Satisfied"

Second: *Knowing how to be satisfied:*

> Knowing how much to take of those things
> which one already has is called "knowing
> how to be satisfied."

The Buddha says: "You monks should contemplate
knowing how to be satisfied if you wish to be liberated
from suffering. The dharma of knowing how to be satisfied
is the realm of riches, comfort, peace, and tranquility.
Those who know how to be satisfied are happy and comfortable even when sleeping on the ground. Those who do
not know, how to be satisfied are not satisfied even when
dwelling in a heavenly palace. Those who do not know
how to be satisfied are poor even though they are wealthy,
while those who know how to be satisfied are wealthy
even though they have little. Those who do not know how
to be satisfied and are always tempted by the five desires
are consoled by those who know how to be satisfied. This
is called 'knowing how to be satisfied.' "

Commentary

As with the last awareness, it's very easy to understand the Buddha's words here. If we know how to be satisfied with the way we are right now, right here, that's all there is to know. This provides an interesting parallel to the last awareness, "having few desires," which meant that among those things we haven't yet obtained we don't want much. Here it says, "Knowing how much to take of those things which one already has. . . " We know how much to take of the things we already have. It is a very wonderful power.

Ordinarily, we are dissatisfied with so many things. If we have dissatisfactions, that simply means we want more than we really need. In one way or another, there is a way to be satisfied with the things we have. If we start wanting things, it becomes endless, and impossible to satisfy ourselves. Then perhaps we come to the point of asking, "If that's the case, what are we supposed to want?"

We are gathering here to practice the Buddha Way together; that's a desire, isn't it? And again we come back to this phrase, "which one already has." We have a certain amount already, and definitely, in addition, there is an appropriate amount to take. Some of us have and use *oryoki*, eating bowls. Our oryoki are considered as important as our life, as Buddha's life itself. That's how we understand oryoki. *O* means "response;" *ryo*, "amount;" *ki* is "container." It's the container which holds the amount necessary to respond to the given need. All of us are oryoki. All of us are containers which carry the necessary amount. Some larger, some smaller. It's not a question of which is right or which is wrong, better or worse. A large thing is a large thing; a small thing is a small thing. That is to say, all of us are the Buddhas, and if we understand that, it is not a matter of being satisfied or dissatisfied. Our life is a totally self-contained, sufficient thing. Becoming aware of this is wisdom.

Even though it's such a simple statement, it tells us a great deal. "Knowing how to be satisfied" sounds a little negative, but it's not so at all. Taking according to our capacity, according to the size of our oryoki, is knowing how to be satisfied. If you have a larger capacity and you put in only a little bit of food, you won't be satisfied. You need to know how much you're supposed to take. Those who have a larger capacity should definitely take more.

Reflecting upon this fact and wondering what sort of measurement we need to gauge our size, I suddenly remembered that Harada Roshi used to talk about the degree of aspiration, what we really want and how much we really wish to accomplish. That's a very good way to measure the size of your oryoki, of yourself. Don't you think so? Those who really have a profound, compassionate, devoted aspiration, even if they contain the whole world, may not be satisfied. Amitabha Buddha had forty-eight vows, and one of them was a vow to forego his personal accomplishment until everybody is liberated. That's his capacity, and certainly he's never been satisfied. Some people think that Buddhism is very negative and passive, very unproductive: we shouldn't have any desires, we should retreat to a mountain and meditate. But that's not true at all.

In any case, we have to begin someplace, from wherever we stand; and wherever we stand, whatever the capacity we have, we try to practice with our best. For example, if we are crippled and confined to our bed, then that's the only way we can practice at that point. That's how I understand "knowing how to be satisfied."

Now let's reflect upon ourselves again, and upon how desires arise. Last time I talked about the five desires and the six delusions. Desires are one of those delusions. In Buddhist psychology, we divide consciousness into eight different degrees or domains. The first five, the senses, are called pre-consciousness: eyes, ears, nose, tongue, and body (or touch). The most common desires have some connection with these five sense organs. The sixth one is the consciousness which periodically receives the images of sound, smell, taste, etc., into the brain and recognizes or perceives them. The seventh is called *manas*, the I-consciousness. For example, we look at something and are attracted to it and want to possess it. What happens in that process is that first we perceive it, then we react to it as beautiful or ugly, pleasant or unpleasant. Discrimination of this kind carries us into the domain of the I-consciousness.

The eighth consciousness is called *alaya* or "storehouse" consciousness. The alaya consciousness is where everything, all memories, images, ideas and information, is stored. On the one hand it is deluded consciousness, the fundamental ignorance which prevents us from seeing the world as it is. And on the other hand it is awareness, prajna wisdom itself, by which we can see that all phenomena are in themselves empty. Enlightenment turns that fundamental ignorance into prajna wisdom and allows us to see that from the very beginning we are the Buddha-nature itself.

In order to be satisfied we should know ourselves, but until we really come to that point we can't be satisfied. Knowing ourselves, even though our body, our existence, is finite, we can see that our life is nothing but the life of the whole world. We are the Dharma ourselves, the Dharma we already have. So in fact, as we live our lives, as we live the Dharma, we each consider how much we are supposed to take. We just know how to be satisfied. It's a very simple topic and yet, if we think about it dualistically, it's not at all an easy thing to do. In any case, the more we understand ourselves, the more we know how to be satisfied with our life.

Discussion

Sensei: "Knowing how to be satisfied" means using what we have in its best way. So what are dissatisfactions? We're all dissatisfied in some way or another with something. What are these dissatisfactions? Why are we dissatisfied?

Q₁: Trying to change karma, I wasn't satisfied where I was, so I came here. Ideally we should be satisfied with wherever we are, shouldn't we?

Q₂: On the other hand, it's all right to leave. Either way. If you stay it's fine; if you want to look for something, that's fine, too.

Sensei: You talked about karma. What do we mean when we say "karma"?

Q₃: Specifically, there are many ways that it's interpreted in Buddhist texts, and I think the most useful is the meaning of "what binds you, what's holding together your particular nexus of circumstances." Why am I here? Why am I related to this situation and these people? That teaches you how your mandala or your sphere of being is, and gives you a feeling of why it is and what you are. Your karma would be your binding tendencies.

Q₂: As I understand it, when you're in the realm of karma you're subject to cause and effect, and the enlightened man is one with cause and effect, whatever happens. In other words, as long as you think there is something wrong with it, you're bound by it. It doesn't mean you can't change it or leave it but it's just a different feeling about it. Acceptance as opposed to resistance.

Q₄: Can you accept it and resist it at the same time?

Q₂: Sure.

Q₃: Sensei, how do you find it useful to look at karma in your life?

Sensei: In one sense, the very essence of life itself is what's meant by karma. In the most general sense, karma is what's happening. It's the very fact that things happen and cause other things to happen, and that all of those things occur or manifest or appear in the way that we perceive them right now. We're all gathered here together and there are many causes and effects that go into that. There is the fact that we've somehow found out about the Zen Center. There is the fact that this seminar was set up. There's even the interest that made us want to look into Zen, into Buddhism, in the first place. There is the fact that this building was bought and this room was made into a seminar room. There are many causal chains, all manifesting themselves in the fact that we're talking here right now. All of that is what's called karma.

In a way, karma is just what's happening, there's nothing fixed to it. Somebody could get sick now or the room could fall down. Everything's constantly changing, and, in a broader sense, that very change is called karma. Sometimes we look at ourselves and talk about personal karma. We start thinking of reasons: Why am I in Tennessee? Why am I on the farm? Why do I read? Why am I at the Zen Center? We look at our stream of life, and trying to figure out why we are doing all this, we say it's our karma. But that gets a little tricky because then we're reducing it to a much smaller sphere, eliminating the biggest sphere, which is also part of us. If we look at it in terms of "my" karma, we fall into one of the traps which Buddhism warns us against, getting caught up with our own ego, with our own individuality. Karma is never that simple. We can't isolate ourselves, we've got to look at the whole thing, because that whole thing is ourselves. That's why karma becomes, in a way, a hard thing to pin down. What it means to examine karma is to get rid of the notion of the smaller self and to see everything in its entirety. Then seeing that, we need to see how everything interacts with everything else. Those interactions, those relations between things, start giving us a feeling for karma.

But from our standpoint the key thing is to realize that karma is ever-changing; it is never constant. It's completely opposed to the notion of possessions or fixed places, and it's not some constant force that can lead us from one place to another. As soon as we look at where we're at and pin it down to a certain place or state of mind, we're trying to regulate it, and all of a sudden we're stuck in our limited, conceptual thinking. That's when problems arise. Just accept the karma that is, accept life as it's flowing, and there can't be any problems. Just go along with it and do what you have to do, not trying to stop it or fix it at some point, which in any case can't be done.

Q: Does Buddhism ever use the words *fate* or *fated*, or does it always just talk about karma? Because I think a lot of people use *karma* and *fate* synonymously.
Sensei: No, *fate* to me has too strong a feeling; it's more deterministic. In Buddhism both free will and determinism exist at the same time. You could say, "Because of what we do, we cause effects, we've got cause and effect going." But at the same time, we have free choice at any moment to do whatever we want. I think it was Rabbi Akiba, a famous Jewish sage, who said, "All is determined, but free will is given." Fate, I think, leaves out that complete freedom.

Q: I don't understand how I'm supposed to know what is the "right amount" of action to take.
Sensei: If we look at our own body, for example, the hand can pick up a lot of things. But if we try to pick up things with our foot, we have a harder time; it picks up much less. The two parts of the body have different potentials for carrying things, but that doesn't make one better than the other. It means they're different. Walking on the feet is much easier than walking on the hands. We tend to accept the limitations of the functioning of the parts of our body, yet we expect other people to be like us and to have our capacity for doing things. We don't accept the potential or the capacity of each person; we don't see what their container is. However, we should always look at these things in an active and a passive way. Being what we are, having the container we have, we should fully use our own potential. Then the question is, How do we determine that? When are we driving ourselves crazy by saying we should be doing more? When are we being too nonchalant by not doing enough? How do we figure our own "size?"

Q: I put in months of waiting on that kind of question; nothing much came out. Somewhere down there (*pointing to his lower abdomen*) I think I know. There is a place there which says "Yes, that's sufficient." I'm often thinking that, and at the same time wondering, "Is this sufficient or not?" If there is even a question in my mind, the answer is already there. There seems to be a native wisdom in a person that says, "If you think that you might be tired, then you're tired, you know." The message has gotten through.

Sensei: Kando, how do you know your size?

Q: (*panting*) When I do that I know I've had enough.

Sensei: But what happens if other people that are helping you are doing that before you?

Q: You have to be sensitive to other people's feelings but still you have to leave it open to them to learn when they've had enough. You can't baby them, you can't always be concerned about whether they're stretching themselves a little too much. But if it's obvious that they're straining themselves, then you've got to help them out in some way.

Sensei: What gives me an uncomfortable feeling is that there is an implied separation in what you say between yourself and others. The mouth sees a lot of food, but the stomach can't eat it all. What is it that looks at food and says, "I want to eat more"? Eventually the stomach gets full, but the mouth says, "Oh, I'll have a pizza. I can get that one in, too." You know that the stomach is full but you're saying, "Let the stomach worry about its problems. It's got to say something; it's got to throw up. I'll wait until I hear from it." Or perhaps you want to carry some load and your arms are getting tired, but you decide to wait until they collapse. If you're in the position of having people working with you, you've got to look at it not as "people working with me," but as "me working." You can't do more than "yourself," which includes all the people involved.

It's interesting. From my own experience, this feeling of knowing when to be satisfied or when not to be satisfied is really very strongly tied up with knowing our own capacity in its broadest sense. If we underestimate our capacity and stop too soon, we get dissatisfied. If we overestimate our capacity and do too much, we get dissatisfied. Underestimating leaves a feeling of, "Why aren't I doing enough?" Overestimating, "Why am I driving myself crazy and running myself down?" We must see our own capacity and our own potential. If we're aware of the fact that we're running ourselves down or that we're not doing enough, then that's one way of sizing ourselves, of seeing what our capacity or our potential is. Being aware of those dissatisfactions can tell us more about who we are and where we're at, and make us more aware of the dissatisfactions of all of us. If we're married, we can be aware of the satisfactions and dissatisfactions of husband and wife and kids as a family. We can be aware of the satisfactions and dissatisfactions of people working with us, and can see the capacity of that unit. Then we can enlarge our perspective, and become aware of the satisfactions, capacities and potentials of everyone we come into contact with.

As our way of practice, zazen is the key to sizing ourselves, to knowing how to be satisfied and knowing what we are. It's fascinating to see that, based on each of these awarenesses, different schools and different methods have developed. In Zen the emphasis is on the continual practice of zazen, allowing our head-tripping to slow down and these awarenesses to unfold naturally. Again, it's such a simple thing, but it's very hard to do.

TWELVE

"Enjoying Serenity and Tranquility"

Third: *Enjoying serenity and tranquility:*

> Being apart from all disturbances and dwell-
> ing alone in a quiet place is called "enjoying
> serenity and tranquility."

The Buddha says, "If you monks seek joy and peace in
the serenity and tranquility of non-doing, you should keep
away from disturbances and dwell alone in a quiet place.
Those who dwell in quiet places are praised and respected
both by Sakrendra, chief of the gods, and by celestial
beings. Therefore, casting away attachment to yourself
and others, dwell alone in a quiet place and contemplate
the cause of suffering. Those who desire the company of
other people suffer from their relationship with them, just
as a tree will be broken and die when many birds roost in
it. The bondage of worldly involvement will drown you in
suffering, just as an old elephant drowns in the mud
because he is unable to get out by himself. To liberate oneself from complicated involvements is called 'detachment.' "

Commentary

Let's appreciate the third of the eight awarenesses of the great person, "enjoying serenity and tranquility." In modern Japanese, the character *gyo*, which I translated as "enjoy," means "music." Its etymological meaning is the music of drums and strings, something we take pleasure in listening to. "To enjoy" or "to rejoice" is the implication derived from such an origin, so I translated it as "enjoying serenity and tranquility." As a definition of this, Dogen Zenji writes, "Being apart from all disturbances and dwelling alone in a quiet place."

In a way, this passage means just what it says, but when we closely examine it, we find that it also means a good deal more. For example, "being apart from all disturbances;" where is there such a place? And what kind of "disturbances" do we have? "Dwell alone;" what does "alone" mean? What does "in a quiet place" mean? Buddha says, "You monks," but we can appreciate it as if he had said these words to all of us. "If you seek joy and peace in the serenity and tranquility of non-doing, you should keep away from disturbances and dwell alone in a quiet place."

We practice zazen here; *za* means sitting, *zen* is derived from the Sanskrit term *dhyana*, which means "quiet thinking," "contemplation." Making your inner condition quiet is *zen*. Making the external condition, the physical condition quiet is *za*, "sitting." The opposite of both is "running around." A spinning top provides an interesting analogy. When we don't spin it right, it wobbles and rolls around on the ground. But when we spin it right, it stays in one place and doesn't wander. It doesn't mean that the top is not active. When we spin it really well, not only does it stay in one place, but we can see the shape of the top as clearly as if it were standing still and not spinning. Our zazen is similar to that. Many people think that sitting is very inactive, a waste of time, but it is not so. Time-wasting occurs more often when we run around and exhaust our energies. In sitting, we raise our energy so that even our internal organs function more efficiently. Not surprisingly, in such an active, positive state, we enjoy serenity and tranquility.

"If you seek joy and peace in the serenity and tranquility of non-doing . . . " This "non-doing" (*wu-wei*) is another key term. It can be translated in various different ways—"non-doing," "inaction"— but it doesn't mean "not doing anything." It means "doing something without being conscious of doing it, without being separated from the doing." Being one with whatever you do, that's non-doing.

Being "alone" means really being yourself, being serene and calm and undisturbed. Our life is all one life—that's the "alone." If we could really be "alone" (all-one), all our difficulties and problems would not disturb us. Instead, we would become even more courageous and determined to take care of them.

When we read a sentence like this, "Dwell alone in a quiet place . . . ," it seems to be telling us to go to some place in the mountains where nobody lives and make ourselves quiet and peaceful. But I don't understand it that way; I don't think that's really possible. Can you do that? Probably you'd be more disturbed. When night came, wild animals would howl and the wind would whistle. During the day, even the wind blowing the leaves might disturb you. Not having a comfortable place to rest might disturb you. And what would you do to provide meals? That's not the way to make ourselves "dwell alone in a quiet place." Rather, it's a matter of how to make ourselves calm and serene wherever we are.

There's a famous poem usually attributed to the Rinzai master Daito Kokushi, who, according to legend, lived for years with beggars under a bridge in Kyoto: "Doing zazen, I see the people passing by on the Fourth and Fifth Street bridges/Like trees in a deep mountain." The Japanese used to wear wooden sandals, and when they walked on wooden bridges it made an awful sound. You can imagine how noisy it would be—horses going by, people constantly walking —and yet for him it was as quiet as living on a mountain. When we realize that everything is nothing but ourselves, then we can be thoroughly "alone."

Hakuun Yasutani Roshi gave me the name *Koun* when I received *inka** from him. *Ko* means "alone," *un* is "cloud." *Hakuun* is "white cloud," and *Daiun*, the Dharma name of Yasutani Roshi's teacher, Harada Roshi, is "great cloud." *Koun*, "lone cloud." I really like that name; blown by the wind, everywhere it goes it's alone. No one can do anything for your life, but your life is everything. Please appreciate this fact, this wonderful life. That's what the Buddha Way is.

"Those who dwell in quiet places are praised and respected both by Sakrendra, chief of the gods, and by celestial beings." All the gods and goddesses in heaven are going to praise you and respect your life. There's an interesting story about Yün-chü Tao-ying (Ungo Doyo), Master Tung-shan's successor, when he was practicing hard, doing zazen alone in the mountains. He used to come back to the monastery at a certain time of the day to eat, but suddenly he stopped coming. After a number of days, he finally showed up and Master Tung-shan asked him, "Where were you? What happened to you?" Master Yün-chü explained, "Devas came down from heaven and offered me food, so I didn't need to come back." Master Tung-shan scolded him, "I thought your practice was even better than that. Devas brought food for you, and praised your practice, but the fact that they recognized your goodness means that your practice is not quite good enough." Master Tung-shan's rebuke is quite another way of regarding the praise of the gods, but here the Buddha says that if you practice well, that is, if you "dwell in a quiet place," even the gods will respect your practice and encourage you.

"Therefore, casting away attachment to yourself and others, dwell alone in a quiet place and contemplate the cause of suffering." "Casting away attachment to yourself and others" sounds very passive and negative, but I don't think it is. We have very complicated human relationships, and I think we can say that in order to make life smoother and more comfortable, human relationships are crucial. In the family, in the community, in the company, and in society at large, the most difficult task is always human relationships. You might say that the difficulty arises because we all have different ideas or thoughts, but if human relations go well, all goes smoothly. Even in government, for example, among Democrats and Republicans, if their personal relationships go smoothly despite different opinions or ideas, the government will be taken care of nicely.

"Casting away attachment to yourself and others, dwell alone in a quiet place. . . . " Interestingly, he actually uses the word "space" instead of "place": "quiet space." That quiet space could be any place. You can make quiet space even in the noisiest place. "Casting away attachment to yourself and others. . . . " If we stop making any distinctions between ourselves and others, attachment in a way disappears. "And contemplate the cause of suffering." The causes of suffering always lie in the distinctions and discriminations one makes between oneself and others. That reminds me of a famous saying of the Buddha: "The three worlds are nothing but my possession, and all living beings are my children." Not only humans, but "all living beings are my children." This seems to be synonymous with becoming aware of this aloneness.

Those who desire the company of other people suffer from their relationship with them, just as a tree will be broken and die when many birds roost in it. The bondage of worldly involvement will drown you in suffering.

Maybe I have been emphasizing the original, intrinsic aspect a little too much. That is to say, all sentient beings are the Buddhas. But somehow until we become aware of it, we can't take that fact as fact. We have to strive to realize it. Then we have to examine ourselves and realize the experiential aspect in actual practice.

Sometimes students who come here are not satisfied with the practice and go off elsewhere to study more. They go to school, to other places, they have contact with many other people, and it creates disturbances for them: "he said such-and-such;" "they are such-and-such;" "I am such-and-such." They return with all sorts of strong ideas, but with no way to resolve those different ideas and live their lives. First of all, we need to face ourselves directly and see where we stand, how much we can do, which way would be the most effective way to practice, and then we have to integrate the many facets of ourselves in order to accomplish the Way, so that we can avoid unnecessary struggle and suffering.

"The bondage of worldly involvement will drown you in suffering." Since Buddha here is talking just to monks, he uses the words "worldly involvement." But when we really appreciate the state of aloneness, there is no distinction between aloneness and worldly involvement. Worldly involvement as such may not be the cause of disturbing your life or practice. However, if we are careless, it is like "an old elephant that drowns in the mud because he is unable to get out by himself." When ten people get together, there are ten ideas and ten ideals, and if we are not strong enough, we'll be drawn this way and that way by the opinions and thoughts of others. Then we can't pursue our practice in an effective way.

"To liberate oneself from complicated involvements is called 'detachment.' " Again it sounds a little negative or passive, but by keeping away from disturbances, you see that "I" is always the one who creates the disturbances, and "I" is always the one who can solve them. Aloneness is nothing but I. We can say, "I am alone in the world," or "I am the whole world." Being so, we can really enjoy serenity and tranquility, since there are no disturbances. Isn't it nice?

Discussion

Sensei: "Being apart from all disturbances and dwelling alone in a quiet place is called 'enjoying serenity and tranquility.'" As Maezumi Roshi said, "dwelling alone" is the key. That is, if we are everything, that's aloneness. In Buddhism, when we talk about being alone, we mean that space in which we are everything. As Shakyamuni Buddha said, "Above the heavens and below the heavens, I alone am the revered one." That "I" fills everything. If there is nothing outside of us, including the thing we're doing, including everything, then how can there be disturbances? So by practice, let's experience this "dwelling alone." Let's be here. Otherwise, wherever we go, it's noisy.

"Non-doing" is being one with whatever you do, doing in this realm of aloneness, or "all-one-ness." In that state, the words *Buddha* and *delusion* aren't necessary. In that state the words *doing* and *non-doing* aren't necessary. It's just what you're doing. If we say, "I'm doing something," already it's dualistic, already it's not this "alone." In that case we can't talk about "non-doing" because we've dipped back into dualism.

Genpo is a very good swimmer. When you become so good at swimming that you're no longer cognizant of swimming, then you are in the state of non-doing. It's an extremely hard thing to be apart from the sphere of all disturbances and to dwell alone. But in a way, that is zazen, that is practice. Let's aim strongly toward this "dwelling alone."

Q1:   Later in this passage it says, "Those who desire the company of other people suffer from their relationship with them. To liberate oneself from complicated involvements is called 'detachment.' " How is it possible to be in relation to other people without experiencing their suffering? I feel he's suggesting that you can be with other people in such a way that you do not imbibe their suffering.

Q2:   I don't think he's working on the literal level of people being together in such a way that one does not imbibe the suffering of others. When you dwell alone, when you're unified with everything that's happening in your experience, that is the way to truly be with another. When you separate yourself so that you and the other remain separate, at that point you create the sphere of confusion and conflict and dualism, so that in talking about taking on the other person's suffering caused by the relationship, you're unclear about who you are. That distances you from what's happening. That's where the trouble comes in. And it's also what keeps you from truly being with another person.

Q₁: I'm not satisfied with that.

Q₃: What about the suffering part? If somebody really has a big pain and you're one with them, it's your pain too. Even if there is a slight distance between you, if you care something about them, when they vibrate that way you're going to be aware of it.

Q₂: There's no reason why you shouldn't be.

Q₄: It's no different from being busy. Serenity and tranquility have to be in the midst of busyness and pain.

Q₂: Or sunshine and rain, or male and female, or hot and cold, or whatever the conditions are. That's just what's happening, and you deal with it as appropriately as you can.

Q₄: It's hard to accept that there isn't some trick for avoiding the "bad parts," though.

Q₁: It sounds like the Buddha is saying there's a way of getting out of experiencing suffering.

Q₃: When he says that the bondage of worldly involvement will drown you in suffering, it makes you want to hide away in order not to drown.

Q₄: But he states it dualistically. We've been talking about experiencing others' suffering. That's the realm of duality, of good and bad, up and down. The thrust of his words here is to transcend that duality, not by escaping but by putting ourselves totally into that involvement.

Q₅: When I hit you, what happens?

Q₁: It hurts.

Q₅: That's right. There is no one suffering. Just this "it hurts."

Q₂: A lot of work has been done in recent years in hospitals, especially with people who are terminally ill with cancer and who are in deep pain most or all of the time. The work, from a variety of approaches, centers on training the people to become one with their pain. These experiments have been very successful in that the people who have really involved themselves in the training generally die very differently from the people who have not been able to become one with their pain. It's apparently something that can be learned.

Sensei: The key here is aloneness. Eliminate the distinction between yourself and others. At the moment of being hit, there is no suffering, there is not even knowing that you're hit. At that very moment, there's no distinction and there's no suffering. It doesn't mean that that rock doesn't land on your head real hard. Still, at that moment that's all that there is; you don't think, "Oh, that rock came down and hit me on the head." It's just that pain, that sudden thing. In that state of oneness it doesn't mean that you've rid yourself of all the things you see and feel in a dualistic state. If you see a person on fire, you feel his suffering: he's burning up! But when there's really no separation between yourself and that suffering, there's no "you" left to suffer.

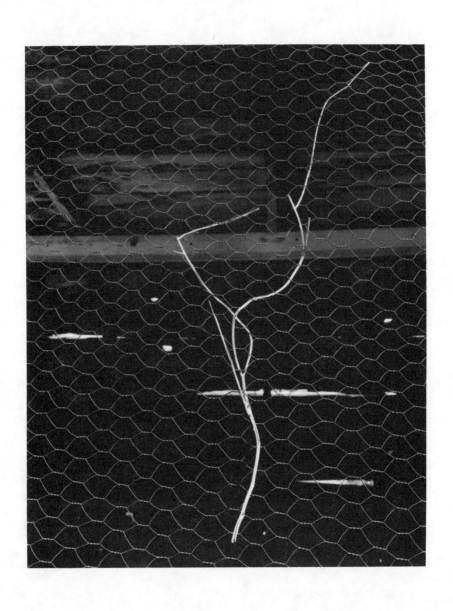

THIRTEEN
"Exerting Meticulous Effort"

Fourth: *Exerting meticulous effort:*

> Exerting oneself meticulously and unceasingly in various beneficial practices is called "meticulous effort." Be precise, not careless; proceed forward, do not regress.

The Buddha says, "If you monks exert meticulous effort, nothing will be difficult to accomplish. Therefore, you should make an effort to practice carefully, for when water flows constantly against a big rock, even a small amount of water will eventually dig out a large hole. But if one who practices becomes lax, it will be impossible to accomplish anything. It is like trying to start a fire by rubbing two sticks together; if you stop rubbing before the wood gets hot, you can't start a fire. This is what is meant by 'meticulous effort.' "

Commentary

When we think about ourselves in terms of our practice, about what kinds of things are necessary to consider in order to have right or meticulous effort, we find that just endeavoring to do something is not sufficient. It should be "right endeavor, right effort," effort channeled in the right direction. But since there are so many alternatives that seem "good" or "right" to us, it is not often clear which direction is the best one to choose.

Relatively speaking, all of us know what is good and what is bad. Yet, in a way, it's ambiguous. A good thing for me to do isn't necessarily a good thing for you to do, and vice versa. What is good or what is bad varies with each one of us according to our varying positions and circumstances, and according to the place and the amount. Then, in terms of our practice, what is the right direction?

Recently I talked about the most important key to our practice: our vows, our wishes and our aspirations. Every day we chant the four vows. They are beautiful vows. As Buddhists, or as people who believe in the enlightened way or the teaching of the enlightened person, every one of us is supposed to make these vows. The first vow is a vow to other people—to save or liberate all beings. The following three are to oneself: to cut down desires; to study and practice well to master the Dharma; then, to attain the supreme Way, realize the supreme Way for oneself. What I want us to appreciate together is the nature of the direction these vows indicate for us. Just "being compassionate" is difficult to comprehend.

In order to discover your own direction, it is important to have great faith in yourself. Believe that Buddha-nature and all kinds of virtues and wisdom are you yourself. See yourself as nothing but the very nature of being. Torei Zenji, a major Dharma successor of Hakuin Zenji, said that if you wish to realize the Way, you must first of all raise great faith. He then outlined ten stages of deepening faith, beginning with the faith that each one of us has the nature and boundless wisdom of all buddhas, and ending with the faith, which comes after one has accomplished the Way, in the importance of continuing and maintaining the stream of Dharma in the future.

Actually, though, the beginning and end of our practice is whether we really believe in ourselves as the Buddha. When you clearly realize that fact, you are truly enlightened. Then there is nothing but the sharing of your realization of yourself as the Buddha with other people. Unless you do that, you can't be compassionate. Seeing yourself as the Buddha, believing and realizing that fact, you can't be anything but compassionate. So I really encourage you to have this strong, deep faith in yourself.

Incidentally, this relates to koan study as well. Koan study is not playing with anecdotes or episodes that happened hundreds of years ago between masters and students. Right now, right here, we have koans, which we work on in order to polish and ripen ourselves, in order to practice meticulous effort. Regardless of whether we are working on koans or not, in one way or another life itself is the koan. We are not studying the koan as such; we are always studying ourselves. Without the koans that someone else set up, we can practice quite well. Making right effort in shikan-taza is again the same thing: have deep faith in yourself, and your zazen will be the same as the zazen of the Buddhas.

Consider the vows—what do we need to accomplish, and how do we accomplish it? First, we raise the bodhi-mind, raise the mind to accomplish *anuttara samyak sambodhi*,* the supreme Way, supreme wisdom. Then we practice, put forth right effort. Then we realize what enlightenment is, who we are, what our true nature or true self is. That's the state of nirvana. In that state, the vows are further nurtured. Then we continue to practice, we realize further, attain nirvana, and then we again renew the vows to accomplish further. I'm paraphrasing the words of Dogen Zenji. Actually, Torei Zenji and Dogen Zenji are talking about the same thing: endlessly accomplishing the Way. Dogen Zenji compares our practice to a spiral, which doesn't necessarily have to be going upward. We can enlarge ourselves in a horizontal way as well. By doing so, we share with more and more people the appreciation of this wonderful, enlightened Way, the wonderful Dharma, the wonderful life of all of us together, which is nothing but each one of our lives. We must clarify our objectives. Then we do our best in whatever way we can; there's no question. That is right effort.

The eight awarenesses themselves are meticulous effort. In the original Japanese, "meticulous effort" is *shojin*. *Sho* is literally "pure," or in Dogen Zenji's words, "being pure, it is not mixed." *Jin* is "progress," or as Dogen Zenji expresses it, "going forward, it does not regress." That is what effort is. Just constantly keep on going.

Here the Buddha says that right effort is like a small amount of dripping water. When it drops unceasingly, eventually it makes a hole in the stone. In another analogy, he compares it to making fire by rubbing two sticks together. If you stop before you get fire, regardless of how hard you try, you will never succeed. In a way our practice is the same. But after getting fire, what are we going to do? There are always further stages to advance to.

The eight awarenesses are interesting. Want little, know how to be satisfied, and enjoy serenity and tranquility. Then with satisfaction, contentment and serenity, further and further, more and more, we just endeavor to advance toward anuttara samyak sambodhi—not only by ourselves, but with everybody.

Discussion

Sensei: As Buddha says, if you keep rubbing two sticks together, even though it seems like you've been doing it for a very long time, eventually the fire will start. Our practice is as sure as that. Consistency.

Q1: What does consistency mean? What about all the doubts that go through your head, back and forth, back and forth, wasting your time? Is that breaking the consistency?

Q2: That's not breaking consistency. Being consistent is, for example, getting up every morning and sitting, then going to work and coming home, eating dinner with the family, then doing something at night. Doing that constantly, continuously, day after day, month after month, without deciding one day, "I'm not going to sit," and another day, "Today I'm going to sit all day." Just be consistent. When people ask me how much they should sit, I just say, "Pick a time, about fifteen or twenty minutes a day, but be consistent about it, and do that every day, five or six days a week. Don't sit one day for two or three hours and not sit for another week. Just be consistent, whatever your practice is. Don't be flighty about it."

Sensei: It's nice to be consistent in the right direction. How do you know the right direction? You can feel it. In Buddhism we talk about looking at four basic elements—time, place, person, and amount—and realizing that those four elements are always changing. But having considered those four key factors, you finally just have to feel what the right direction is for you. And it's important to realize that what's right for you is not necessarily right for me. We're two different people. What's right to do in the library isn't necessarily right to do in the zendo; they're two different places. What's right to do now isn't necessarily right tonight when we're going to have a party; different places, different times. One person may like to sit for hours and hours, but that's not necessarily right for somebody who is just starting to sit and is going to be in pain. We just don't have a standard which applies to everybody.

Q₃: In relation to consistency, doubt is one of the major hindrances if, everytime you have a doubt, it pulls you away from your practice.
Q₂: Yet it doesn't necessarily mean you can't be consistent.

Q₁: Is doubt the same thing as lack of faith? This is something that really concerns me.
Q₂: I think "faith" is one word that bothers people who are beginning to think about practice. It brings up visions of believing in something whether you understand it or not.
Sensei: We talk about three major prerequisites for practice: faith, doubt, and determination or perseverance. Those are the three qualities that Harada Roshi mentioned as essential. Now we all have different amounts of each of those. If great faith is your strong point, then usually your practice is not koan study but shikan-taza. You don't need anything to drive you; you've got this really strong faith. Very few people have it. Faith in what? Faith in yourself. Faith in the fact that, "Yes, I am Buddha, I am the Three Treasures. Why do I need koan study, why do I need gimmicks or techniques?" It's all resolved, because you've got this tremendous faith. But how many people have that? If you do, then where is the doubt? If you don't have doubt, you'll be consistent in your practice.

Now the second prerequisite is doubt. "What is all this that they're talking about? They're saying I'm Buddha. I know I'm not Buddha, but I want to be. I want to find out what that means." Now that's what led Dogen Zenji. He didn't have tremendous faith. He had tremendous doubt. He wanted to know. They write in all of the sutras, which are the recorded teachings of Shakyamuni Buddha, that everybody, as he is, is Buddha, Buddha-nature manifesting itself. But even Shakyamuni Buddha practiced for many years before he realized that. So we have this conflict: on the one hand we're Buddha, and on the other hand we've got to practice. What does that mean? Shakyamuni himself had serious doubts about that, which drove him to practice.
Q₃: But he still had faith that what they said had value, that the practice they set out was going to lead to a result that he wanted. That's a tremendous amount of faith.
Q₄: Yes, he always had faith in zazen.
Q₅: We really trip a lot on the adjective *great* in the phrase or *great faith*. "Great" describes the faith we have, when we flick the light switch, that the lights are going to come on. We don't think, "My

God, I have this incredible faith thing going with the electric company." We just flick it on and we're surprised if it doesn't come on. It's not incredible; it's everyday faith, only applied to a very fundamental issue instead of to something as superficial as an electric light switch. We're applying it to ourselves and saying, "Wow, I really know I am the Way."

Q4: You don't have to make as much personal commitment to turning on the lights as you do to putting your body and time into zazen, into just that initial first five years or so of physical and mental agony. I really appreciate my own faith. I'm amazed at discovering how much faith I have. I've had important experiences in my practice, but they've faded and I've never really understood what has kept me going.

Q5: We don't need to tell ourselves that we're working all this hard for something that's really rare and elusive. We're working all this hard for something that to us is as common as dirt.

Q3: But then I have to believe that what I'm working on, what I'm doing sitting on this cushion, is going to lead to the result I'm interested in. That's the faith I'm talking about. Do I really think that by sitting here on this cushion every morning for five, ten, fifteen or even twenty years, I'm going to be self-accepting and know who I am and my place in this world?

Q5: There's no guarantee, but you'll never know if you don't try it.

Q: You talked about great faith, doubt, and consistent practice. Can you also talk about drive?

Sensei: Actually drive is the third aspect we're talking about here. Because we don't have enough faith in just doing what we're doing, and because we do have doubts about what's happening, then we have to have the determination to resolve those doubts. If you don't have the determination to resolve this, you'll just read some books and be satisfied. The reason we get into this kind of practice, or any kind of practice, is because we have this determination to resolve our doubts.

Q: I'm wondering whether it's possible that what Shakyamuni Buddha meant by practice here is something much more general, much broader than mere sitting.

Sensei: Right. We don't say practice is zazen. Zazen is the core of the practice, but that's not the only thing we do. Ours is a full practice. When we say the word *practice*, we mean much more than zazen.

Q1: When you said, "Take what you can handle" in the discussion on "knowing how to be satisfied," could you also apply that to the kind of practice, as well as to the length of time you sit?
Sensei: I think so.
Q2: I think there is another aspect to that too: take what you can handle and maybe just a little bit more. Push yourself a little bit; not unrealistically, but if you can sit easily for fifteen minutes a day, try twenty minutes. Give yourself a little nudge.
Sensei: My own feeling is that if you're consistent in your practice, then there are a couple of things that will happen. Either it turns out to be the wrong practice for you, or it will be the right one for you, and you'll go on.

To get back to great faith in ourselves, it seems to me that one of the ways of getting that great faith is by studying ourselves. You know the famous words of Dogen Zenji, "To study the Buddha Way is to study the self. To study the self is to forget the self. To forget the self is to be enlightened by all things." The more we study the self, the more we forget the self, and the more we have this great faith in ourselves. Some people just have it; that's their karma. Each one of us has a different amount of faith, a different amount of doubt, a different amount of drive, a different amount of consistency. But the deeper we go into ourselves, the more we raise that great faith, until it's not something we can even call faith. As Daishin said, you turn the light on without thinking of it as faith.

Let me also mention again those four aspects of practice that Roshi referred to earlier: raising the bodhi-mind; practicing; attaining enlightenment, realizing the Supreme Way; then throwing away that realization, and again raising the bodhi-mind, practicing and attaining the Way. That to me is a definition of "exerting meticulous effort." It encompasses everything we've discussed so far. Definitely, doing that, you'll enjoy serenity and tranquility, even though everything is going on with all its goods and bads.

Q1: Realizing and going on—is that something like realizing the oneness, then purposely seeing the differences?
Sensei. We're going to talk about oneness and differences a little later on, but in this case it's just realizing—anything—then throwing it away. Throwing it away is at least as important as realizing it. Just

drive on until you come to some new insight, some new realization, but don't stop; throw it away and go on.

Q₂: When you throw it away, is that the same as forgetting it?

Q₃: Yes. Get rid of it; don't be attached to it.

Q₄: There is a specific kind of forgetting: not misplacing it, but making it so much a part of you that you no longer need to remember it.

Sensei: It is also important in terms of meticulous effort to renew our vows each time. In a way they can help to raise the bodhi-mind. Every night when we end sitting, we chant: "Sentient beings are numberless, I vow to save them. Desires are inexhaustible, I vow to put an end to them. The Dharmas are boundless, I vow to master them. The Buddha Way is unsurpassable, I vow to attain it." If you really put yourself into those vows, you have to raise the bodhi-mind. Raising that bodhi-mind, you have to practice. And practicing, you have to realize. But then don't stop, just throw it away. Right effort is encouraged by a group practice with a teacher who is capable of really teaching. It gives you something to check in with, to bounce off of, to get feedback from. "What needs particular attention at this point? Am I going off center?" Through that contact you start to develop your own sense of when you are on course and when you're not.

FOURTEEN

"Not Forgetting [Right] Thought"

Fifth: *Not Forgetting [Right] Thought:*

> This is also called "maintaining right thought."
> "Protecting the Dharma and not losing it"
> means "right thought," or "not forgetting
> [right] thought."

The Buddha says: "If you monks seek both a good teacher and good protection and support, nothing is better than 'not forgetting [right] thought.' For those who do not forget [right] thought, the robber-like multitude of deluding passions cannot break in. For this reason, you should always keep right thought in your mind and regulate it well, for if you lose this thought, all sorts of merits and virtues will also be lost. If the power of this thought is strong and firm, then even though you mingle with the robber-like five desires, you will not be injured, just as, if you go into battle dressed in armor, you will not fear the enemy. This is the meaning of 'not forgetting [right] thought.' "

Commentary

In Japanese, "not forgetting [right] thought" is *fumonen*, "do not forget the thought." For this *nen*, we use the English equivalent "thought." What is that thought? You might think that it is the same term we use when we chant the passage in the *Heart Sutra*, "form is exactly emptiness, emptiness exactly form; feeling, thought, discrimination, awareness are likewise like this." But that "thought" is different.

More and more I have become aware of how important words and expressions are. For example, Buddha says of "not forgetting [right] thought," if you really have right thought, it is like going into battle with armor. You can't get hurt. What kind of armor is it? What kind of fight is it? What kind of enemy is it? An analogy is always partial; we can't cover everything with one analogy. We should really understand what Buddha is talking about here and at the same time, practicing the Buddha Way, we should really understand what the enemy is; what the armor is; who has to wear such "protective armor" and from what kind of attack we have to protect ourselves. More precisely, we have to understand that there is no need to wear armor or to protect ourselves from anything.

Then what is that armor? It's yourself. Yourself, myself—the same. Each one of us could be the strongest armor that nothing could destroy, and on the other hand, each of us could be our own worst enemy. Not anybody else, anything else outside of ourselves. That's what Dogen Zenji says: "To study the Buddha Way is to study the self." We could be robbers, or animals, or hungry ghosts, or fighting spirits. We could be buddhas or bodhisattvas. "For this reason, you should always keep right thought in your mind and regulate it well."

These eight awarenesses expressed by Dogen Zenji are the same awarenesses that Shakyamuni Buddha left for us when he left this life. And that was the same teaching that he taught the first disciples after his attainment at the age of thirty-five. He talked about the eightfold path, the sixth one of which, "right thought," is defined as "maintaining right thought" or "protecting right thought." That is what is meant by "not forgetting thought." Buddha taught various principles, teachings, anecdotes, analogies, and all those teachings are the Dharma. If we take a step back and look at those teachings, we can see that they are also the Three Treasures, the very foundation of the Buddha Way. And what are the Three Treasures? Almost half of you have had jukai. Each time I give jukai, I say the Three Treasures are nothing but yourself. To really maintain and protect them is not forgetting right thought. As long as you really protect and maintain them, everything else will follow quite naturally. Just be one with the Buddha, Dharma and Sangha; in other words, really be yourself.

Each of us has a different position, different work, different status, different appearance, and yet each of us is exactly the same in the sense that each of us as an individual is the absolute, is the Buddha Tathagata. If you don't accept this, you are forgetting something; you are ignoring something; you are not maintaining right thought; you are not protecting right thought. If you really maintain this right thought, you are wearing the strongest armor, and you don't need to wear anything to protect yourself. Being yourself, just maintain this "not forgetting [right] thought."

In order to illustrate this point, let me again quote the famous koan about Yen-yang and Chao-chou. Yen-yang asked Chao-chou, "How about one who has nothing?" (Nothing to protect, nothing to wear, no enemy, no one to be harmed, then what?) Chao-chou said, "Cast it away." Yen-yang asked further, "Having nothing, what is there to cast away?" Chao-chou answered, "If so, carry it on." Reflecting upon ourselves, what is there to carry, what is there to cast away? Again, I have to come back to the same point: let us be the Three Treasures ourselves. Then being so, we'll know what to wear, what to protect, and what to trim off.

As I mentioned earlier, the word translated here as "thought" is *nen* in Japanese, and the character *nen* consists of two parts: the top part means *ima*, "right now, at this very moment," and the bottom part is *shin*, "mind." The mind of this very moment, that's *nen*. Don't forget the mind of this very moment. Protect the mind of this very moment. Maintain the mind of this very moment. For example, coming to the zendo to sit, what kind of mind, what kind of thought do we have? Protect it, maintain it and don't forget it.

I think Suzuki Roshi took the inspiration for the title of his book, *Zen Mind, Beginner's Mind*, from a passage of the *Avatamsaka Sutra:* "The very beginning mind itself is the most accomplished mind of true enlightenment;" or, "The very moment of raising beginner's mind is the accomplishment of true awakening itself." We also have a common saying in Japanese: "Do not forget the beginner's mind." When we really understand that, beginner's mind is beginningless mind. Then we just maintain and protect it. Again, when we become aware that beginning is beginningless, in other words, the beginning is also the end and the end is the beginning, then without artificially trying to do anything, our life goes smoothly. That is not forgetting [right] thought.

Discussion

Sensei: Let me preface this discussion with a few words about the Three Treasures. As Maezumi Roshi has mentioned, "not forgetting [right] thought" means to remember that we are the Three Treasures. Twice a month, during *fusatsu* (renewal of the vows), we chant, "*Namo* Shakyamuni Buddha," which means, "Be one with Shakyamuni Buddha," or simply, "Be Shakyamuni Buddha." Be Manjusri Bodhisattva. Be Avalokitesvara Bodhisattva. Be one. In jukai the first thing we say is "Be Buddha, be Dharma, be Sangha." Those are our basic vows. But since we already are that, we are really saying, "Remember that we are the Three Treasures."

There are three ways of looking at the Three Treasures. The first is called "the Three Treasures of one body." In this way of looking at the Three Treasures, everything as it is is the Three Treasures, there's no division. Everything is contained right here, right now: all space, all time. Everything is *just this*. The whole universe in space and time, all thoughts, all actions, all phenomena, everything going on is just this one body. If we look at it in that way, then there's only one treasure, just this, and that's us. I am everything. Everything is nothing but me.

Then when we say "Three Treasures"—Buddha, Dharma, Sangha—we're splitting this one thing up into three things. Buddha is the unity, the fact that there is only one thing. Dharma is the multiplicity of phenomena, the fact that there are numberless things, numberless beings, and each one of them is different. And the Sangha is the harmony, the intimacy, the fact that unity and difference exist simultaneously without interfering with one another. All together Buddha, Dharma, and Sangha are just different ways of talking about the one reality, which is nothing but ourselves, nothing but our life.

The second way of looking at the Three Treasures is called the "manifested Three Treasures." Unless there is someone who realizes the one-body Three Treasures, it has no value, and so the historical Shakyamuni Buddha is essential. His teachings are called the Dharma, and his disciples, the people studying with him, are called the Sangha. In this way, the Three Treasures are manifested in space and time.

The last of the Three Treasures is the "preserved Three Treasures." The teachings have to be transmitted from generation to generation, and so we have all the enlightened teachers and their teachings, and all of the people down through the ages who gathered around them to study. Of course that includes Maezumi Roshi and his teachings, and those who practice with him.

The primary implication of this fifth awareness, then, is to realize and to remember what the Three Treasures are. It's amazing—we could brainwash ourselves into thinking we were the Three Treasures, but a week later we would forget.

The second implication of this awareness is that although zazen is the core of our practice, we have to study and remember what we've studied. Beginning students often believe that there shouldn't be any study, that we should just sit, but in fact there's a tremendous amount to learn. Having a firm foundation in the teachings, we should practice without forgetting and without being attached to what we've learned.

Q: It really struck me when you said that if you wish for a good teacher, then consider "right thought." When I first came here, I remember how being around Maezumi Roshi was a way of remembering what I was about without busy-mindedly thinking about what I should be doing. A teacher is like right mindfulness. He really helps us to make "right thought" part of our total being, not just an intellectual concern.

Sensei: Definitely that's true, and Shakyamuni Buddha is also saying a little more than that. He's saying that if you want to practice, if you want a good teacher, if you're looking for protection and support, nothing can be better than remembering that you are the Three Treasures.

Q: What is that remembering, though? It's not just an intellectual thing. It's remembering with our total being, right?

Sensei: Right.

Q: In the beginning it's hard. We might accept it intellectually but we really need a teacher.

Sensei: I definitely agree with you. But he's saying nothing is better than realizing who you are.

Q: Amen.

Q: I'm not clear on something. It seems that what we're talking about here is holding onto mindfulness, which essentially is being completely one with what's happening at the moment, being filled by the thing so that there's no separation between us and it. Am I right about that?

Sensei: My understanding of this word *nen* is that it's not straight mindfulness as you just described it, but that it has the connotation of remembrance or recollection. That's why it's translated here as "not forgetting [right] thought." It has the connotation of knowing something and carrying it with you, without letting it slip away. In the ten precepts, the last precept is: do not abuse the Three Treasures, do not speak ill of the Three Treasures. The implication of that precept is that if you forget that you are nothing but the Three Treasures, then you are abusing the Three Treasures.

We also talk about two ways of breaking the precepts once we've received jukai and vowed to maintain them. The first is when we just violate the precepts, which is happening at every moment. For example, the first precept, "do not kill," applies to everything: insects, plants, bacteria, even molecules. Every time we breathe, we destroy molecules and change them to other things. We eat food; we wear clothes; we step on the ground and kill microscopic organisms. We are constantly killing things, yet we vow not to kill. In reality we violate all of the precepts at every moment, and all we can do is appreciate what we are violating and why we are violating them. It's like dirt that accumulates in our cup; we can always wash that cup. We have to drink, we have to dirty that cup, and so we are constantly washing it clean.

The second way of breaking the precepts is to destroy the precepts, to break the vow, to break the cup. We do that by losing faith in ourselves, forgetting that we are nothing but the Three Treasures, nothing but Buddha, Dharma, Sangha. Not just to have weak confidence or to think that we're not doing so well, but to have a complete breakdown, a complete loss of faith in the value of our lives. He says here, "If the power of this thought is strong and firm, then even though you mingle with the robber-like five desires, you will not be injured."

At the basis of all of this, of course, is the state of just being one with the present moment, which is called the "great rebirth," the functioning of enlightenment. So really "being one" with this moment is great enlightenment, which is to know you are the Three Treasures.

It's very easy to use statements such as "everything is as it is" to lead to all types of philosophies. Beat Zen developed on this very idea: if we are mindful and if we are one with this very moment, then there's no problem. But there's more to it than that; we have to realize and never forget that we are the Three Treasures, and let that be the basis from which our actions spring. Not that it's something that we're attached to, but that it's ingrained in us that this is what we are. Then being one with this moment, we will be moving in the right direction.

Recently, Maezumi Roshi compared faith to a steering wheel. He said if we don't have that steering wheel and we just put our foot on the gas-pedal of determination, we'll lurch ahead blindly and bang into all sorts of things. But maintaining right thought, remembering that we are nothing but the Three Treasures, we can give our vehicle as much gas as we want to give it, and we'll be headed off in the right direction.

Q: Several weeks ago I was reading about this "not forgetting thought" and felt very much at one with the ideas expressed. Then for the last two weeks I've been involved in a very difficult work situation, and have been wallowing in a lot of negative feelings. Just before coming to the zendo tonight I was reminded that the discussion was going to be about "not forgetting thought," about not forgetting that you are the Buddha, Dharma, and Sangha, and I realized that that's exactly what I had been doing. I had been forgetting, and even more precisely, my mind was being robbed by a desire for money, material things, and fame. Now I'm being reminded that I am the Buddha, that I am the Dharma, and that I am the Sangha, and I want to say that, from my experience, forgetting that can be very messy.

Sensei: First of all, though, we have to know what it means when we say that we are the Buddha, Dharma and Sangha. If we don't know what it means, there's no way for us to remember it. My saying it, or Shakyamuni Buddha's saying it, or Dogen Zenji's saying it, or Maezumi Roshi's saying it, or even your saying it, won't mean a thing if you don't know what it means. And if you really know what it means, you won't forget it.

Q: I don't feel like there are only two speeds, though: knowing what it means and not knowing what it means. I say this because I don't know what it means all of the time, but some of the time I do. I think that there are glimpses and degrees.

The Hazy Moon of Enlightenment   125

Sensei: I would definitely agree with you that there are degrees of understanding. That is, each one of us in this room has some idea of what it is, and yet nobody in this room really knows. There are many ways of looking at it, and in fact, "What are Buddha, Dharma and Sangha?" is a lifetime question for us. As we practice, our ideas will change, and hopefully they will finally converge.

FIFTEEN

"Practicing Samadhi"

Sixth: *Practicing Samadhi:*

> Dwelling in the Dharma undisturbed is what
> is called "samadhi."

The Buddha says: "When you monks unify your minds,
the mind is in samadhi. Since the mind is in samadhi, you
know the characteristics of the creation and destruction of
the various phenomena in the world. For this reason, you
should constantly practice with diligence and cultivate all
kinds of samadhi. When you gain samadhi, the mind is
not scattered, just as those who protect themselves from
floods guard the levy. This is also true for practice. For the
sake of the 'water of wisdom,' then, cultivate samadhi
well, and do not let it leak out. This is called 'samadhi.' "

Commentary

Let's consider samadhi together. In this passage Dogen is using
the term *zenjo*. Originally the word *zen* came from the Sanskrit *dhyana*,
which was phonetically rendered into Chinese as *ch'anna*, and eventually shortened to *ch'an* (J: *zen*). *Dhyana* originally meant "quiet
thinking" or "contemplation;" by contemplating certain objects or

subjects, one learned to concentrate. Samadhi (*jo*) is the state of concentration itself, the state in which subject and object are one. In the eight awarenesses, practicing dhyana or samadhi is the sixth one. In the eightfold path it comes last. There are other words in the Indian tradition that denote this kind of concentration, for example, *yoga* and *samapatti*, and in fact, various degrees of samadhi were recognized and named. Buddha is saying in this particular article that you should practice different kinds of samadhi.

In our daily life we frequently experience samadhi, the state of concentration, of becoming one. We can observe samadhi in our work, in our study, in watching television or in thinking. There is even the samadhi of gambling. It's rather easy to get into the kind of samadhi where we are absorbed in whatever we are doing. We call that "samadhi in the realm of desire." We speak of three worlds: the realms of desire, form and no-form. These worlds are not geographically or spatially located; all exist in our mind. That is, the state of our mind can be described in terms of the three worlds. In the *Diamond Sutra*, it says that the three worlds are created by the mind.

Theoretically speaking, what kinds of states of mind are these? The realm of desire is the normal state of mind in which we live. We have senses and consciousness, and we relate ourselves to the external world under the influence of conditioning created by our senses and consciousness. When we see something, we are conditioned by what we see. Our hearing, smelling, tasting, touching and consciousness are the same. We are very easily conditioned by thinking and so create all kinds of problems and frustrations. Strictly speaking, we don't call these conditioned states "samadhi," even though they are concentrated states—for example, forgetting ourselves while watching a movie.

In the next stage, the realm of form, strong attachment to the discriminative senses and consciousness disappears. I don't know whether it's correct to explain it in this way, but you become more genuinely spiritual, yet you are attached to the existence of certain objects, though in a much more refined way.

The third realm, the realm of no-form, is still more refined and is even further divided into four different stages. The samadhi in these two realms, the realm of form and the realm of no-form, is called "fundamental samadhi." This is the samadhi we are in when we are genuinely involved in practicing, when we can sit and concentrate well. Beyond that, there is one more state of samadhi which is called "the samadhi of no leaking." In other words, not even the slightest attachment to any thought remains. These are very technical descriptions and not especially helpful from the point of view of practice. In any case, we should be aware that there are many different levels and kinds of samadhi.

Now to practice Zen, what kind of samadhi should we have? One of the phrases the Chinese used to translate the Sanskrit *samadhi* was *cheng shou* (J: *sho ju*), literally, "right receiving." By concentrating well, we still the waves of the mind and are able to see things clearly, as they are. What causes these waves is the wind of our thoughts and ideas. Of course, there is nothing wrong with this wind, but when we stick to it, it becomes the cause of difficulties and troubles. The practice of samadhi eventually cuts out the root or source of this wind itself. Perceiving externals as they are, we naturally know how to respond to situations. This is "right wisdom," which flows spontaneously out of deep samadhi. As the Sixth Patriarch Hui-neng says in the *Platform Sutra*, "Samadhi itself is the substance of wisdom; wisdom itself is the functioning of samadhi."

Unfortunately, our concentration, our samadhi power, is usually not that good, and up to that point we experience many stages or degrees of concentration which we also call samadhi. In that sense, we can also say that samadhi is the state of mind prior to wisdom.

Interestingly enough, in the eightfold path or the Buddha's eight awarenesses or the six paramitas*, the three most fundamental elements of our practice are sila (precepts), samadhi and prajna (wisdom), in that order. In the eightfold path, the last one is not right wisdom, but right samadhi. Usually, however, we add two more stages to the eightfold path: right wisdom; and right liberation, true freedom and peace. Wisdom always comes after samadhi. It is a logical thing, and as a matter of fact, it actually happens in that way.

At any rate, knowing that there are many different degrees of concentration, we encourage ourselves to concentrate well. Ideally we should concentrate all the time, whatever we do, wherever we are. In this way, we can increase our samadhi power more and more, and then some chance happening will make us aware of our wisdom. As a matter of fact we are using our wisdom all the time, but we are just not aware of it.

Usually we understand ourselves as very unique and special, distinct and separate from externals, as if we were in a dream. That is "I." "I am different from anybody else, anything else." All kinds of subject-object relationships are established. Not only human relationships, but relationships to everything. We say, "this is mine; that's yours." Or, "That's none of your business; it's my business." Or, "I think such and such. I am right, you are wrong." Buddha says such upside-down thinking is a delusion, but we don't think so. We believe that what we think is right.

The wisdom we talk about is the vision with which we see equality or oneness. That's the beginning of acquiring wisdom in a different dimension. The enlightenment experience is nothing but awakening to this wisdom, and samadhi makes it possible. In deep samadhi, the subject-object relation is eliminated, and we realize this wisdom.

A magnifying glass provides a good analogy. If we take a magnifying glass and use it to focus sunlight on a piece of paper, eventually the paper will burst into flame. Up until that point, the paper is only hot. But when it starts to burn, the energy is completely changed. Heat has turned into fire.

Now, if we don't focus those rays properly, if the focus is not one-pointed, no matter how long we hold the magnifying glass, the paper won't burn. The same is true of our practice. We can practice zazen for many years, but without strong concentration, our samadhi will not flare up and turn into the experience of enlightenment, which is the awareness of wisdom.

At the Zen Center of Los Angeles, our practice generally takes three different forms: koan study, shikan-taza, and awareness on breathing. Technically, there are many ways to practice. Even within koan practice itself, there are many koans. Whatever problem or difficulty we are facing can be a wonderful koan. Or we can practice by concentrating on a particular object. Because of the personality or characteristics of each person, each of us has certain tendencies. Some get angry easily, some are more agreeable, some more ignorant, some more logically or intellectually oriented. Depending on the person, certain subjects or objects are recommended for concentration. For example, concentration on breathing, one of the five techniques traditonally recommended for focussing the mind, is a very effective practice. It is not necessarily only for those who have just started to practice. Just by following or counting the breath, we can get into deep samadhi.

Important for good sitting is the proper disposition of the body. If you sit with your chest compressed, you can't actually breathe well. So when you sit, the chest cavity is supposed to be open. Let the body sit quite naturally, and you can breathe more deeply and easily. Those who are working on koans must let the mind be occupied by the koan. Then concentrate and get into samadhi. Koan is mind. The same is true for shikan-taza. In this way, we train ourselves more and more, and when the time ripens the flower of wisdom opens.

Therefore, when you sit, please try to sit well and don't make your conscious mind scattered. Whatever disturbs your concentration is makyo, and there are all kinds of makyo. One kind of makyo is scattered, busy mind. Another is dull, drowsy mind. When you sit, you should avoid these two major tendencies as much as possible. Try to sit well, and try not to leak too much. As Buddha says, "For the sake of the 'water of wisdom,' then, cultivate samadhi well and do not let it leak out." Regardless of whether you are aware of it or not, you are the container of wisdom. Don't let it leak. Take care of it well and preserve it well. Then when the time comes, you'll really see how to utilize that wisdom fully, not only for yourself, but for other people as well.

Discussion

Sensei: Most people who talk to me about samadhi think of it only in one of its senses, that is, as very deep concentration. I remember one sesshin I attended where a woman entered that kind of samadhi. It was the first time I had ever seen anyone go into what is clinically called "deep samadhi." She hadn't been practicing for very long, and this was perhaps her second or third sesshin. When she didn't get up at the end of the first sitting in the afternoon, Roshi asked me to let her be, and we intentionally avoided disturbing her during walking meditation. She ended up sitting about five or six hours, through dinner and break, and then, towards the end of the evening sitting, she heard the dokusan bell and got up and went to dokusan. She had no idea how long she had been sitting, and she had no pain in her legs. She just stood up and went to dokusan as if she'd been sitting for half an hour.

Such clinical samadhi is what people generally think of when they hear the term *samadhi*. But as Roshi explains in his talk, there are all kinds of samadhi. For example, we talk about samadhi in the three realms: the realms of desire, form and no-form. In deep samadhi in the realm of desire, we might be playing poker and really watching the faces of the people we're playing with. In our sitting, as we drop off attachment to our desires, we enter into samadhi in the realm of form. Our sitting deepens to the point where we're not distracted or attached to things caused by our senses. It doesn't mean they're not there, but we're not attached to them. Yet still we're aware of ourselves and of those things, still there's something of a split.

But then our sitting goes even deeper, to the point where not only isn't there any attachment, but there's no division at all. A bell sounds; it's just the bell. No "I" exists, nothing separate. There's a story of one roshi who screamed out in pain when the hanging bell was struck to begin a period of sitting. And then there's the story of the monk who was doing zazen in an inn, working on the koan "the cypress tree in the garden," when a robber slipped in through the window to see what he could steal. As soon as he saw the monk sitting on the floor, he screamed out in surprise and alarm and jumped back out the window. All he could see was a cypress tree in the middle of the room. That's called samadhi of no-form. The monk wasn't there anymore, only the tree. This is what Dogen Zenji is referring to when he says: "For the sake of the 'water of wisdom,' then, cultivate samadhi well, and do not let it leak out."

Any kind of attachment at all, any kind of separation, any clinging no matter how small, is called the leaking of samadhi, the leaking of the water of wisdom. "No leak" means that not even the slightest attachment to anything remains. If the monk was aware of being the cypress tree, then his samadhi was leaky. That state of "no leak" is difficult to achieve, and in our koan study, we're asked to present the koan with that spirit. In any case, as we sit, our concentration becomes stronger and stronger, the space between subject and object becomes smaller and smaller, and we experience different levels of samadhi. Yasutani Roshi says that after sitting twenty years you can finally say that you've begun to learn how to sit, and that your samadhi has matured. Many of us will take even longer than that. But in the broader sense, whatever state of mind we're in at any particular moment is our samadhi at that time.

There's a famous koan in which a monk asks Yün-men, "Tell me, what is samadhi." And Yün-men says, "It's rice in the bucket." That is, it's everything that happens during the day—eating the rice, cooking the meal, driving the car, sweeping the floor. So please don't worry about what level of samadhi you're experiencing. What's much more important is our constant practice.

Let's have some questions.

Q: In his talk, Roshi mentions that wisdom is the functioning of samadhi, that actually samadhi and wisdom are the same thing. Could you talk about the relationship between wisdom and samadhi and also the relationship between deep samadhi and enlightenment?
Sensei: It's interesting how for many of the aspects of our practice it can be said that one is the functioning of another. For example, wisdom is the functioning of samadhi, and compassion is the functioning of wisdom. In the case of samadhi and wisdom, a frequently used example is the candle. The lighted candle is samadhi; the light it gives off is its functioning, its wisdom. But you can't differentiate between them. There's just the candle burning and giving off light simultaneously. The light being given off is the functioning of that candle, and the very state is the burning itself. Wisdom in Buddhism has nothing to do with knowledge or intelligence. Wisdom is the functioning of what is.
Q: There must be different kinds of wisdom just as there are different kinds of samadhi.
Sensei: Definitely.
Q: But then what about prajna wisdom? Is that a different kind of wisdom, or is it wisdom in the broadest sense? And then is it an expression of a functioning of a particular kind of samadhi?
Sensei: Just as there are many degrees of samadhi, so there are many kinds of wisdom. We talk about empty wisdom, prajna wisdom, that is, the wisdom of seeing the oneness of all things, which is the wisdom of deep samadhi. On the other hand, if my samadhi is weak and I'm attached to lots of different things, then that's the kind of wisdom that will emerge. Now we have difficulty because we want to think that wisdom is somehow different from our normal, everyday functioning. But the statement "Everything, as it is, is Buddha-nature" means exactly that. Even the state of clinging to things is Buddha-nature, and the functioning of that state is wisdom. Enlightenment is just the experience of realizing that fact. In a way, it's a very simple fact, but we don't want to accept it. Somehow we expect wisdom or Buddha-nature to be something special, something more.

As for the relationship between samadhi and enlightenment, we say that the depth of enlightenment depends on the depth of samadhi. This is only natural because enlightenment or insight is just becoming aware of the state that we're in. Usually, we have a first "opening" early in our practice, when our samadhi is not that deep.

Then we study koans to clarify and polish that first insight, until at some point we have another, much deeper realization. We then no longer have any doubt about why we practice, or what direction our practice should take. But even at this point, if we stop practicing, our realization will fade, and our samadhi will leak away.

Samadhi is like a reservoir. When we sit, we're filling that reservoir, and as the reservoir gets fuller and fuller; we become more and more stable, and more and more able to live our lives with confidence. Naturally insights will arise, and we have to let those insights go and continue our practice. Otherwise, we become attached to our realizations, and our samadhi dissipates.

Q: Many arts and practices, particularly the martial arts, center on cultivating *joriki*, the "power of samadhi." In tai ch'i or aikido, for example, this flow of energy is usually called *ki*(Ch: *ch'i*), and it is very important to be able to develop and use that ki. How is our practice different in its balance from such practices, which emphasize the cultivation of joriki?

Sensei: We call people who practice in this way joriki freaks, samadhi freaks. They appear in Zen practice too, and they'll probably criticize me for not being one. But our practice is essentially a letting go and a going on. That doesn't mean we don't generate deep samadhi, but that's not our particular goal or direction. It's a by-product, not something that we're trying to do, or that we attach to. We don't stop at any particular inn, for example, the joriki inn, and build up its reputation. Our goal, if any, is to be completely free. This means that at the same time that we can develop our samadhi and use it to become a fine painter or a fine aikido master, we have to let go of our attachment to that samadhi and go beyond it. Again, if our powers of concentration are only available for one particular art or discipline, that's not Zen samadhi. In Zen, our power of samadhi should function twenty-four hours a day, throughout our life.

Q: Trying to use this samadhi in my life, when I started practicing I could see concretely that my ability to relate to people or situations seemed to be very responsive to the quality of my sitting. When I'd reach a barrier, I'd always feel that the barrier was something in my sitting, and I'd try to resolve it by sitting more. It was a very different experience for me when I tried to resolve the barrier by just really staying with and working with that situation, letting go of the idea that the best way to resolve it was to increase my samadhi.

Sensei: I think that's true. I think, though, that what's also important is to practice consistently so that our samadhi, our stability, just keeps steadily improving. I often hear people say, "I used to sit really strong, I had tremendous samadhi, and now nothing seems to work right." But those same people are the ones of whom you'd say, "Their practice has become so solid over these past few years." When we look at ourselves, we can't see ourselves over the span of a few years. We are only aware of our faults, and think, "I could be doing so much better." In fact, the stronger our sitting becomes, the more clearly we see the weaknesses and limitations of our practice. It's an endless process. And the key is just to sit consistently, and little by little our concentration will develop, our samadhi will deepen, and our joriki and stability will increase. Then when those situations come up, we can handle them better. To run away and sit rather than face them—that's not the answer.

Q: What's the relationship between different practices such as shikan-taza or muji or koan practice and different kinds of samadhi?
Sensei: Certain koans, like "the cypress tree in the garden" or "muji," are very similar to shikan-taza and following the breath in the kinds of samadhi they build. Then there are other koans which aren't oriented that way at all, which are more concerned with improving the way we express our understanding.
Q: So a practice that emphasized shikan-taza or breathing would be a practice which emphasized samadhi?
Sensei: Yes. Koan study is a mixture, whereas those other practices more directly emphasize building samadhi. Ultimately, however, the difference is one of emphasis.

In 12th Century China, there was an ongoing debate between the "silent illumination" sect of Zen, headed by Master T'ien-t'ung Hung-chih (Tendo Wanshi), and the "koan" sect, headed by Master Ta-hui Tsung-kao (Daie Soko). The one stressed samadhi, while the other emphasized insight, satori, realization, and the arguments on both sides were often quite heated. Yet when he died, Hung-chih named Ta-hui to succeed him as head of his monastery. The differences between the two teachers never obscured the basic realization which they shared.

SIXTEEN

"Cultivating Wisdom"

Seventh: *Cultivating wisdom:*

> Wisdom is aroused by hearing, reflecting,
> practicing, and realizing.

The Buddha says: "When you monks have wisdom, you are without greed. Always reflect upon yourselves; do not lose this wisdom. In this way you can thus attain liberation in my Dharma. One who does not is neither a follower of the Way (monk) nor a white-robe (layman), nor is there any other name for him. True wisdom is a stout boat which crosses the sea of old age, sickness and death; it is also a great bright torch in pitch black ignorance; a good medicine for all sick people; a sharp axe which fells the tree of delusion. Therefore, by means of this wisdom which is heard, reflected upon, and practiced, you will increase your merit. When one has the illumination of wisdom, even though one's eyes are merely physical eyes, one is a 'clear-seeing person.' This is what is meant by 'wisdom.' "

Commentary

As always, the Buddha speaks of wisdom using analogies, and in plain, simple words. He says, "When you have wisdom, you are without greed." We suffer because our desires are not fulfilled, and greed occurs because of ignorance. From a Buddhist point of view there are three poisons which disturb us: greed, anger and ignorance. When we examine these three poisons, all can be traced to ignorance. Because of our ignorance, we experience anger and greed, which are the opposites of compassion and generosity. Here he talks about how we can turn that ignorance into wisdom: by hearing, reflecting and practicing.

Briefly speaking, there are two kinds of wisdom. First, there is the wisdom which still has some leak; it's not complete wisdom, but partial wisdom. And then there is complete wisdom without any leak, which we gain by attaining enlightenment. Of the first kind of wisdom there are four modes, three of which are mentioned right here: the wisdom of listening; the wisdom of reflecting; and the wisdom of practicing. There is also a fourth innate wisdom which we have from birth: even without learning anything, we still know how to get milk from our mother's breast.

By listening we try to understand the nature of our life, the nature of our practice. When we listen we usually listen having our own opinion or criticism. When listening to someone else talk, we place ourselves against what they say, which decreases the effectiveness of listening. Instead, when we listen we should just really listen, just put ourselves totally into it and try to be one with what is said. In that way we direct ourselves toward the supreme enlightenment which is anuttara samyak sambodhi.

Then, after listening carefully, we should carefully consider what we have heard or read. Just thinking is not enough, regardless of how well we think, or of how good our ideas are. Then we have to put it into practice, we have to confirm ourselves as wisdom itself, which is what we are doing. However, just practicing, even though it is wisdom, is still not yet complete wisdom; all these are still forms of the wisdom which has some leak. By really realizing what Buddha says by ourselves, we turn it into the wisdom of no leak.

What is unique to Buddhism is this awakening. Other religions seem to depend on some almighty figure or idea, but there is no almighty in Buddhism. Recall the famous expression, "When you meet the Buddha, kill him. When you meet the patriarchs, kill them." We don't particularly recognize any authoritative existence. To become awakened, to become aware of the true face of life, is Buddhism. Then what we find is not at all difficult to explain. As I always say, find out the sphere of oneness, find out that there is no division between ourselves and externals. To actually see this is wisdom.

According to another Buddhist theory, there are four kinds of wisdom: great, mirror-like wisdom; the wisdom of equality; the wisdom of subtle observation; and the wisdom of the senses, which in our daily life we are using from morning to night. As I mentioned in my talk on the second awareness, in Buddhist psychology we divide our consciousness into eight different parts or levels. The first six are the senses, which in Buddhism include conscious awareness. The seventh one is *manas* consciousness; the eighth one is *alaya* consciousness. The eighth turns into mirror-like wisdom, the seventh turns into the wisdom of equality, and the sixth turns into the wisdom of subtle observation. The five pre-consciousnesses, the senses, turn into the wisdom of communication with the externals, the wisdom of seeing, hearing, smelling, tasting and touching.

But somehow in our life, these wonderful consciousnesses do not function as wisdom. We don't see all as one; we separate externals and ourselves by having the idea or thought of "I": "I am something different from you. I am not paper. I am not Buddha. I am not sun. I am not tree." But what is "I?" It's what we call manas consciousness, the seventh consciousness. Actually, such a thing doesn't really exist, but somehow we firmly believe there is an "I," which is the very cause of our problem. By our practice, by sitting, or by concentration, we try to cut off this false, deluded idea of "I." Dogen Zenji says in the *Shobogenzo Genjokoan*: "To study the self is to forget the self." In order to examine ourselves, we have to study ourselves, and actually that is Buddhism: ways to study the self. When we forget the self, what happens? We are enlightened by all things. That means we become one with everything. Then being so, we realize the wisdom of equality. We see the nature of all being, not only of ourselves, not only of others, but of everything: that is kensho.

Then again, when we really see that nature from an entirely different standpoint, we appreciate all phases of existence. No two things are exactly the same; everything is different. Even two identical, blank pieces of paper are totally different. Even two specks of dust are totally different. When we see these differences, that's the wisdom of subtle observation.

When we see that sameness is nothing but difference and difference is nothing but sameness, that one is all and all is one, that's the great, round, mirror-like wisdom. Then whatever we see, whatever we do, becomes the expression of wisdom. That's what we call the wisdom of communication with externals. Having such wisdom, we can go on with life regardless of what hardships we have.

> Always reflect upon yourselves. Do not lose this wisdom.
> In this way you can thus attain liberation in my Dharma.

In its largest sense, everything is the Dharma. There is so much to say about this word *Dharma*. In its narrowest sense, Dharma can be understood in two ways: as the sutras that the Buddha expounded; and as the content of those sutras. We can also divide the Dharma further into certain categories according to content. The first one includes all kinds of Buddha's teachings; we generally speak of 84,000 dharmas. In these he expounded the law of causation, the causes by which we will attain supreme enlightenment. Certain causes brought us to be here, as we are, in the life we are living. All is causation; that's one way of looking at the Dharma.

Another important aspect of the Dharma is that it is completely empty; everything has no fixed substance as such. If we think of ourselves, there is no such thing as "I," no human essence, no object essence, no fixed substance or entity. All is constantly changing. There are many ways to understand the Dharma. In fact, one of the four vows we chant each evening is, "The Dharmas are boundless, I vow to master them." To see clearly that the Dharmas are boundless, and to continue practicing to master those Dharmas, is wisdom.

> One who does not is neither a follower of the Way (monk),
> nor a white-robe (layman), nor is there any other name for
> him. True wisdom is a stout boat which crosses the sea of
> old age, sickness and death; it is also a great bright torch
> in pitch black ignorance; a good medicine for all sick people.

In a way, all Buddha's teachings are like medicine. Good doctors are the ones who really know precisely what the sickness is and can prescribe the most effective medicine in the appropriate amount. Recovery is then fast. As a matter of fact, there are four different ways that Buddha expounded the teachings. One way is very general: what he said is true for everybody. Secondly, he taught according to the needs of each particular individual. The third way literally means "the teaching of giving medicine": knowing the precise cause of suffering, Buddha taught the remedy for it. Then the last one is the first principle, the essential truth beyond all skillful means. Buddha spent all his life expounding the Dharma, but waited over forty years before really talking about this first principle.

Like the Buddha, we must have patience and diligence in following the Way; in fact, such patient practice itself is nothing but the cultivation of wisdom. When the time comes, the flower of enlightenment will bloom, and yet that is not the end—our practice continues forever. It's all medicine. Let's continue to take that medicine, and diligently cultivate our wisdom together.

Discussion

Q: Would you consider our preconceived ideas and value judgments as a part of I-consciousness?
Sensei: Yes, all the opinions and ideas that we have which make us separate from others are part of what we define as "I." If we didn't have any of those, then it would be very hard to find this "I."
Q1:   When a person gets into deep samadhi, he doesn't realize that he is sitting there, entirely peaceful and tranquil. I wonder which consciousness he is in at that point? Is that mirror consciousness or pure consciousness?
Q2:   It could be mirror wisdom but it could also be just a state of dullness. It really depends on how it functions as to whether it is wisdom at all or whether it's simply a kind of dull state.
Q3:   I really have faith in what the Sixth Patriarch said. Samadhi and prajna are not two different things, especially if we have faith in shikan-taza. The closer we get in sitting to honing things down, the closer we get to washing that dish or to scratching our nose. Life is an unending samadhi, so in sitting there can be any of these wisdoms. In any of our active moments, when we're not on the cushion, it can be any degree of samadhi.
Sensei: Another thing I think we always have to realize is the state-

ment that Shakyamuni made, "How wonderful, how wonderful, all sentient beings have the wisdom and virtue of the fully enlightened one." That is, pure wisdom is how we're functioning, how the senses are functioning. We eat, sleep, sit zazen, do all kinds of things. We talk about these stages of samadhi as ways of looking at our progress or at the practice, but really, what's the difference between our functioning and the Tathagata's functioning, the Buddha's functioning? Of course, when we say there is none, that's not entirely accurate either. But if you say there are differences, what are they?

Q: It seems to me that what I learn in practicing is to maintain my attention. That's what seems to be the point. It seems to me that the longer one practices, hopefully, the more one can maintain this level of attention. I notice that Roshi doesn't miss things; I miss about 90%. Both bodies are functioning but there is an enormous gap in my awareness. I suspect that gap exists in other people. If you're totally aware, then you see what's going on and you can really function effectively.

I would like to ask a question, though. I get into two kinds of sitting; it seems to me they both help me but they are totally different. One is where you tend toward shikan-taza and you become very aware of everything. Hopefully, there is nothing that gets by, at least for a short period of time. The other kind of sitting is where the sensory world begins to fade, and keeps moving further and further away so that you have more and more nothing. They seem in a way to be totally different. I sit both ways depending on what I'm trying to do. Can you comment on that at all?

Sensei: It seems to me that you're talking about two kinds of samadhi. My understanding of sitting in Zen is that it should be the first kind, one should become really aware.

Q: I don't necessarily choose the second, but sometimes I can be trying so hard to maintain this alertness that before I know it, it's slipped away. Is that bad sitting?

Sensei: No. You know how to sit, and it's not necessary to be constantly questioning or worrying about how your sitting is going. I know for myself that, when I sit, each time is different, each day is different. When I sit I just sit, and it goes however it goes. To try to figure out whether it was a good sitting or bad sitting or the right way or the wrong way isn't really the point. I think if you keep sitting and are consistent, you need not worry about whether it's right or wrong, good or bad, the sitting just naturally deepens in strength.

144   Cultivating Wisdom

Q₁: I'd like to make a comment on wisdom and patience being the same, and then your later statement that everything we do is wisdom.
Sensei: That's a nice question.
Q₁: I can't feel that when I'm being impatient, I'm wise.
Sensei: When you say that, though, you're using the word *wise* the way we use the word *smart*. Wisdom is not that kind of thing.
Q₁: Am I in a state of wisdom when I'm being impatient?
Sensei: Prajna wisdom is seeing things as they are, and the functioning of wisdom, therefore, is the functioning of things as they are. So you could say that being impatient is nothing but the functioning of wisdom. Prajna wisdom is nothing but seeing and realizing that things are as they are and then functioning that way. We're using that all the time. Sitting here like this is the functioning of wisdom. Throwing up is the functioning of wisdom. It's got nothing to do with being smart or dumb. Dumbness itself is the functioning of wisdom. But I didn't answer your question, How is that the same as patience?
Q₂: The thing that strikes me is that as long as I separate myself from what's happening, then I can't really be patient. I can force myself to keep quiet, I can sit on myself but I can't really be patient. As soon as I can simply be one with what is going on, then there is no need for patience, patience is an essential part of what's happening. Of course, that's also the same as the wisdom of equality. So the starting point of patience is that first step.
Sensei: It's interesting, another name for Shakyamuni Buddha is "he who is able to be patient." The wisdom of subtle observation, of seeing the differences, is seeing the fact that things are going at their own pace, and are happening the way they have to happen. For example, we can't expect a tortoise to be running at the speed of a greyhound, but if we make the mistake of thinking all things are the same, then we may ask, Why isn't that tortoise running like a greyhound? Right here at the Zen Center of Los Angeles, there are different people with different capacities to do things. If we really see those differences, right there is patience. But if we have some idea of how they should be and expect them to be other than they are, that's the opposite of wisdom and that's where impatience arises. We're impatient because we can't see the differences between things.

Similarly, we're impatient with ourselves because we can't acknowledge that our pace is different from somebody else's pace, our capacity is different from somebody else's. We may think, "I want my zazen to be free of thoughts," and so we get impatient. But subtle observation is seeing, "This is what I am." Seeing that, we just sit, just act, and this becomes pure wisdom, or functioning wisdom. Just happening. Just sitting.

Q: If each consciousness contains all of the eight consciousnesses, then how are the six senses contained in the *alaya* consciousness?
Sensei: Can you show me a place where one of these eight levels of consciousness exists by itself? For example, can the I-consciousness be isolated from the other seven and function by itself? What are we describing? Dogen Zenji says, "To study the Buddha Way is to study the self." We're studying the self, so we really can't separate these eight consciousnesses. We can talk about them separately, in just the same way that we can talk about different parts of speech if we want to diagram a sentence. It's expedient means. Categorizing has meaning and value, but ultimately it's just one thing that's happening. So of course, in that sense, they are all contained in one another.

Q1:   I always think of the I-consciousness as turning into the wisdom of sameness, so in a sense, the discriminative functioning disappears.
Q2:   I hear you asking, "Doesn't the discriminative functioning vanish when that I-consciousness is transmuted into wisdom, the wisdom of equality?" I would answer that that's the process described in saying, "First there is a mountain, then there is no mountain, and then there is."[1] At the point where there is no mountain, the discriminative part is eclipsed or suspended because what's happening primarily is that you and the mountain become one, there is no separateness. As you move beyond that, once again there is a mountain, there is a return of the discriminative function, but on a very different level and coming from a different place.
Sensei: In terms of what we've been talking about here, what I said originally was that this I-consciousness becomes the wisdom of equality, which leads directly to the wisdom of subtle observation. Seeing the differences is that discrimination you talked about. First seeing the oneness, then seeing the differences from the standpoint of oneness; we can't stay stuck in the realm of the wisdom of equality. We have to see that both are nothing but the same thing, two sides of the same thing; that's the mirror-like wisdom. Then we go past that and drop all traces of any kind of wisdom or non-wisdom, and

we're just functioning the way we're supposed to. But it's quite different now. That's pure wisdom.

Q2: If we interrupt that process at any point it will no longer continue. If we start grabbing hold of one aspect or one stage of it and say, "Now I am at this stage," then that act in itself causes the wisdom to turn back into ignorance. That kind of understanding then becomes makyo because it gets us stuck in one static place.

Sensei: The koan you're talking about is to try to prevent this "stickiness." A person comes along and asks me my name, and I say, "I'm Kando." Then you say, "I'm Tetsugen," and I say, "I'm Tetsugen, too." That is being one with everything to the point where I'm everybody. I'm Tetsugen, I'm Ryogen, I'm Helen, or Helen's me, it's all one state. That's all right, but you can't get stuck there. It's also true that I'm Tetsugen and that's Helen and that's Kando. You must see that oneness and difference are both true at the same time, and then forget about all of that.

Q1: Are they both true at the same instant?

Sensei: Sure.

Q1: Or are you shifting from one to the other?

Sensei: No, no shifting.

Q2: In that respect there is also no such thing as separate instants.

Sensei: My hands are me, right? My hands are also my hands. Both are true at the same time. It's not that at one instant my hands are me, and at another instant they are my hands. What's the difference between the first and the third sentence? We say first a mountain is a mountain, then it's no longer a mountain, then it's a mountain again.[1]

Q1: Supposedly we go through some authentic change to look at it now in a different way.

Sensei: What's this authentic change?

Q1: I don't know. Why do you suppose I'm sitting?

Sensei: What is this change? Does the mountain change from green to purple?

Q1: No, my attitude changes and comes from a different place.

Sensei: How does the attitude change? It's a key matter. Having gone through this phase of the wisdom of equality, we've changed the base on which we're standing. Before having kensho, before seeing the oneness of things, certainly we see all the differences: this is me, that's everybody else, all the different things are there. Then we experience oneness, we find out what it is when we say that everything is Buddha-nature, we realize what this Buddha-nature is. This then becomes the basis upon which everything operates. Seeing the differences then becomes what we call subtle observation, instead of just ordinary observation. When we express it in words, it sounds the same. We still say, "I'm here and you're there," but there has been a big qualitative change. To make that subtle change, we have to experience the wisdom of equality. What we mean when we say kensho is not to discover a Buddha, not to get something that we don't already have, but just to see the Buddha that's been there all along.

Roshi spoke about four wisdoms: mirror-like wisdom, wisdom of equality, wisdom of subtle observation and pure wisdom. First, the kensho experience transforms the I-consciousness into the wisdom of equality. Then comes the wisdom of subtle observation which corresponds to our conscious brain, then the mirror-like wisdom corresponding to alaya-consciousness, then the last wisdom corresponding to the first five pre-consciousnesses or the senses. He's translated it as "pure," but the sense of it is "manifested wisdom" or "functioning wisdom," although the Chinese character doesn't have such a complicated feeling. It's more like the very fact that the eyes see, or the ears hear. I think the reason he used "pure" originally was because there is nothing extra added; just the very functioning of our senses. When you walk, you walk. It doesn't have any of the smell of this wisdom of equality. When we talk about these other wisdoms they are like something special, like phases that we go through, but then finally it's all quite natural.

SEVENTEEN

"Avoiding Idle Talk"

Eighth: *Avoiding idle talk:*

> Having realization and being free from dis-
> crimination is what is called "avoiding idle
> talk." To totally know the true form of all
> things is the same as being without idle talk.

The Buddha says: "When you monks engage in various
kinds of idle talk, your minds are disturbed. Although you
have left home [and become monks], you are still not liberated. Therefore, you monks must quickly abandon mind-
disturbing idle talk. If you would like to attain the joy of
the extinction of delusion, you must first simply extinguish
the affliction of idle talk. This is what 'avoiding idle talk'
means."

Commentary

In Japanese the title reads *fukeron*. *Fu* is "negation," *ke* means "to
play with," *ron* is "talk or argument," or, in broader terms, any writings, principles or discourses. We should remember that this teaching

is the very last teaching of the Buddha; after expounding all sorts of complicated principles, he finally talks in such plain words as these. Therefore, we should carefully consider what he really means, and what each of us usually understands by "idle talk."

As the definition of "avoiding idle talk," the text says, "Having realization and being free from discrimination is what is called 'avoiding idle talk.' " The term *sho*, which I translated as "realization," means also "to confirm" or "to verify," to verify by our whole being what life really is. By doing so, by being so, we can be free from discrimination. Otherwise, as long as we talk about things as if they were outside of ourselves, our talk will be idle. In a sense, that is why Buddha mentions this "avoiding idle talk" last. It is the result, the fruit of our wisdom. Only after we have overcome the fundamental delusion of a gap between ourselves and others can we really avoid idle talk.

This reminds me of the famous story about Yen-t'ou (Ganto) and Hsüeh-feng (Seppo) in which Hsüeh-feng attains enlightenment on Mt. Ao. These two men were close Dharma brothers under Master Te-shan (Tokusan). One day they got caught in a snowstorm while crossing a mountain pass and had to wait in an old cabin for the snow to stop. Hsüeh-feng spent the time sitting in zazen, while Yen-t'ou, who had already attained great enlightenment, napped and took it easy, and teased his elder brother for his serious practice. Hsüeh-feng could only reply that somehow his mind was not yet at ease, that he was not quite confident of his own understanding.

Yen-t'ou then asked Hsüeh-feng to recount the important enlightenment experiences he had had in twenty or so years of practice, offering to check them for him and to approve or disapprove them. After listening to Hsüeh-feng tell of his three "breakthroughs," Yen-t'ou finally commented, "Whatever comes in through the six senses is not the real treasure. It should come up from inside yourself and cover heaven and earth." Hearing this, Hsüeh-feng at last attained great enlightenment, and, dancing around the hut, cried out repeatedly, "Today Hsüeh-feng has attained enlightenment on Mt. Ao!"

Everything that comes from outside of us, from someone or someplace else, through reading, through hearing or through seeing, will be a kind of idle talk unless we really understand the very nature of our own being, of our life. Understanding our life, we will then understand everything else as Buddha-nature itself.

Of course, in the strictest sense, everything we say is idle talk.

Before enlightenment or after enlightenment, to the extent that life is life, we have to speak dualistically. Remember the famous words of Ch'ing-yuan Wei-hsin (Seigen Ishin): "For thirty years before I had penetrated Zen, when I saw mountains, they were mountains; when I saw rivers, they were rivers. Later, after I had intimately met my master and gained the entry point, when I saw mountains, they were not mountains; when I saw rivers, they were not rivers. But now that I have attained the state of essential repose, when I see mountains, they are just mountains; when I see rivers, they are just rivers." What we say and what accomplished people say is in a way the same, and yet there is a difference. By realizing or confirming it for ourselves, our talk will not be idle. "To know true form exhaustively is to be without idle talk." The English words "to know" seem too weak; there are all kinds of knowing. In the original it says *gujin*, a word which Dogen Zenji used quite often. *Jin* means "exhaustively or thoroughly." *Gu* means "clarify completely." "True form" is another key Buddhist term which has the sense of "true reality" or "true wisdom." What is the real face of life? By being discursive, we can't fully realize it. We must thoroughly clarify it in actual practice.

We can also approach this in a positive way and in a negative way. In the negative way, we can try not to spend time on idle talk. Being aware of what we say, we can avoid unnecessary talk, or talk that creates a sense of a gap or separation from others. In a positive way, we can talk in a way which is not idle. This again relates to eliminating the fundamental dichotomy of subject and object. It is interesting that Buddha himself purposely avoided talking about certain subjects, for example whether the universe is or is not eternal, or whether the Buddha exists or doesn't exist after death. These came to be called in Sanskrit *avyakrta*, "undetermined," or in Japanese, *mu ki*, matters it was "no use" arguing over. In this regard, Buddha was fond of telling the story of the man who was shot with a poison arrow. Being shot with a poison arrow, wouldn't he be wasting his time to ask where the man who shot the arrow came from, what color his eyes were, or what kind of bow he used? His first concern should be with pulling out the arrow stuck in his flesh. In the same way, Buddha only concerned himself with matters that benefited other beings and helped them toward realization.

Verbal expression is perhaps the most effective, important form of communication, and involves more than the voice. Writings can be idle talk. Our own thinking can be idle talk. Even our zazen is filled with idle talk, right? Regarding speech, it is important to consider the way we talk, what we talk about, even the quality of our voice itself.

A number of you have had jukai. Of the ten grave precepts, ten guidelines or aspects of our practice, four concern speech: do not tell a lie; do not be ignorant; do not discuss others faults; and do not praise youself and blame others. That is how important right speech is in our practice, in our life. But above all, the point is to realize that non-discursive, non-discriminative life altogether as a whole. When we do that thoroughly, it is called enlightenment.

Buddha says, "Although you have left home [and become monks], you are still not liberated," simply because you are bound by discrimination and are not free from dichotomy. "Therefore, you monks, must quickly abandon mind-disturbing idle talk. If you would like to attain the joy of the extinction of delusion, you must first simply extinguish the affliction of idle talk." That's what we are trying to do when we do shikan-taza or work on muji. We are trying to realize the extinction of delusion. That is what it means to be without idle talk.

It is nice to see that we are practicing and growing together. I really hope that you'll thoroughly accomplish your practice. By doing so you can benefit not only yourself and the people around you, but also many other people. In connection with this eighth awareness regarding speech, let us be mindful. Living together, let us try not to say anything which might harm or hurt other people or destroy our practice. Let us be kind and helpful and pursue our practice together.

Discussion

Sensei: We talk about two kinds of expressions in Zen: dead and alive. Using dead talk, we express our understanding in a dead manner so that the one who listens holds onto what we say as an idea or a concept. In this way, we hinder their realization. That's the problem with all the talks we give, and why everybody is so reluctant to talk too much. Most of the time our expressions provide new ideas to attach to.

An alive expression is one in which we don't give the person anything to hold on to, but rather something which forces them to re-evaluate what they've been doing, or to see it in a different light. An alive expression can be verbal or non-verbal. Somebody coming along and hitting you with the kyosaku* can be a very alive expression which frees you where you're stuck. For example, the kyosaku may knock you out of your nice, confident sitting. This can be done verbally also, by learning how to express what you realize in an alive, helpful way.

Another way to judge whether your talk is idle or not is by whether it is improving or disturbing the harmony. *Sangha*, which is often translated as "harmony," can be looked at in several ways. If we look at the Sangha as the people studying here, then harmony is the relations between the people studying and working together, and idle talk would be talk that interfered with or disrupted that harmony. We can also look at the Sangha as being the relationship between phenomena. When we see the Dharma as all the things that are happening and Buddha as the supreme Way, the oneness of everything, their harmony is the interrelatedness of all phenomena, the fact that it's all one thing manifesting in many ways. To see that harmony is mirror-like wisdom. To disturb that harmony is to hinder the possibility of another's seeing the way things are flowing together, for example, by giving them some idea or philosophy to attach to.

Q1: But how can you really interfere with that harmony?

Q2: Those precepts are good examples; elevating yourself by criticizing others, or talking about others' faults.

Q3: It happens, you know. For example, somebody will be upset with what is going on, and will go around complaining rather than doing something about it. This upsets the harmony of the Sangha.

Q1: But in some sense even that doesn't feel like interference.

Q3: It may or may not be. In a sense, you could say that nothing can upset the harmony, everything is in balance, even when it's out of balance. But in another sense, you can say that idle talk is upsetting to a Sangha.

Sensei: We always have to look at it from both sides. From the intrinsic standpoint, we're all Buddha, and the Dharma is everything, no matter what we do. The Sangha, the harmony, is simply the relationship between things as they are. From the experiential side, we have to practice and there are things that we can do. We can take these precepts to heart. What it boils down to is that I'm everything, so if something goes wrong, I have to look at where it has gone wrong in me, and what I am going to do about it. As soon as I start blaming others for it, something is wrong. No matter how much it seems to be their fault, that's not the place to look. If we truly see that we are everything, then these precepts become expressions of just what is. As long as we don't see that, then we go around blaming others and hurt the harmony, hurt the Sangha.

Q: Extending what we're saying right now about the harmony and Sangha relations, can you give me a little story or an example that will tie it in with the idea of "avoiding idle talk."
Sensei: Eliminate the self.
Q: But you said something about experiencing the talk. I really don't understand that.
Sensei: I'm using the word *experience* in the same way as *realize*. Realize who we are. That is, forget the self and be enlightened by all things.

Q1:   You seem to extend the word *talk*. Do you also intend to include as talk musicians playing music and artists drawing or sculpting?
Sensei: I would say, instead of using *talk*, use *expression*; "avoid idle expressions" encompasses a great deal.
Q2:   He's also talking about thinking itself. He says, "Having realization and being free from discrimination." That would involve every function, not necessarily just talking or other external forms of expression.
Q3:   Again, there are two ways of looking at it. If you take it in a more specific sense, almost everything we do is idle talk or discrimination. And if you take it in a general sense, then you could say that nothing we do is idle talk. Everything is just an expression of our Buddha-nature; everything is perfect as it is. Then talking about something is fine.
Q4:   To find a middle ground between those two, a sense of appropriateness is really helpful. There are times when talking about practice is really idle talk. It's easier to tune into a situation and be appropriate when you're not all wound up in yourself, in your appearance and ideas.
Q5:   How about just plain wasting time talking? You know how you get together with a bunch of people, you're sort of half tired, and you sit around and talk about nothing.
Q2:   That may be why he's described this as idle talk. Often if we're discriminating between ourselves and others, we use talk as a way of cushioning, of making that relationship smooth, of trying to block

and hide the discrimination. That's idle talk.

Sensei: But Hotei* did a lot of "idle talking."

Q2:   It wasn't idle talk in that case because he was enlightened.

Q3:   So are we.

Sensei: I like the word *appropriateness*. And I also love to talk.

Q1:   In the book *Cutting Through Spiritual Materialism* there is a chapter on the bodhisattva vow that says that compassion and communication are one and the same thing.

Sensei: I think so. If you're really compassionate, there's no way you could not extend yourself to communicate. Communication can take many forms but being compassionate certainly means having to communicate. Somehow, some people come to the conclusion that the best thing to do is not to talk at all: whatever you say seems wrong so why say anything at all. It seems to me that we have to communicate, but everybody's idea about how to do that is different.

Q1:   Just show friendliness.

Q2:   Chogyam Trungpa Rinpoche has another phrase I like, "idiot compassion." There are people running around being nice mostly for their own sake. It seems really important to cultivate the wisdom to know how to be compassionate, and then to practice being more skilled at it.

Sensei: We say that compassion is the function of prajna wisdom; that is, wisdom and compassion are the same thing. When our expressions are really the functioning of wisdom, then we are avoiding idle talk.

Notes

PART I

1. Translated by Norman Waddell and Abe Masao in the *Eastern Buddhist*, vol. 6, no. 2, October 1973 *(also found in On Zen Practice II)*.
2. "Yen-t'ou's final treatment of Hsüeh-feng." See commentary on the eighth awareness.

"Yün-men's fifteen years of dealing with Attendant Yüan." For fifteen years Master Yün-men said only the following words to his attendant: "Attendant Yüan" and—when the attendant would answer "Yes"—"What is it?" One day, upon hearing Yün-men call his name, Yüan finally attained enlightenment.

"Shoju Rojin's handling of Hakuin." When Hakuin had his first enlightenment experience as a young man, he became very conceited, thinking that no one in the last 500 years had had such a profound awakening. Finally, at the advice of his fellow monks he went to visit Shoju Rojin, who saw his conceit immediately. Shoju Rojin deflated his disciple's pride by giving him one difficult koan after another, finally bringing him to great enlightenment.
3. "Daitsu Chisho Buddha's sitting in the zendo for ten kalpas." See the *Gateless Gate*, Case 9.

"Shakyamuni's twenty-one days of meditation." According to one traditional account, the historical Buddha Shakyamuni continued to sit in meditation for three weeks after his enlightenment, before setting forth to preach the Dharma.

"Te-shan's visiting Kuei-shan." See *Blue Cliff Record*, Case 4.
4. According to the T'ien-t'ai (Tendai) School of Buddhism, Shakyamuni Buddha revealed the true Dharma to his disciples gradually, and reserved the ultimate teaching until the final years of his life.
5. "Donkey or horse with ease." See *Blue Cliff Record*, Case 52. As used here, the phrase means "all sorts of people," even those with no more intelligence than a donkey or a horse.

PART II

1. The *Book of Equanimity* (Ts'ung-jung lu; J: Shoyo roku) is a koan collection of 100 cases compiled in Sung Dynasty China by the Soto Zen master T'ien-tung Hung-chih (1091–1157). Following the example of Master Hsüeh-tou Ch'ung-hsien (Setcho Juken) (980–1052), compiler of the *Blue Cliff Record*, Master Hung-chih wrote an appreciatory verse for each case. Several gen-

erations later, Master Wan-sung Hsing-hsiu added a preface and a long commentary to each koan, and composed capping phrases (*jakugo*) for the main case and appreciatory verse. We have included all but the long commentary to "Yün-men's Two Sicknesses" here.

2. "Capping phrases." Even when a student of Zen has grasped the meaning of a koan intuitively, his teacher may still require him to present a capping phrase (*jakugo*) to sum up his intellectual understanding. The capping phrases for this koan were written by the Sung Dynasty Zen master Wan-sung Hsing-hsiu (see note 1, above).

3. The one who "takes meals" has a sickness so subtle that he doesn't even know he needs medicine.

4. "One-piece enlightenment." A term here used in the sense of "all-pervading". Sometimes used to mean "one-sided."

PART III

1. See commentary on the eighth awareness.

GLOSSARY

(Editor's note: Although we have chosen not to use macrons in the text, we are including them in the glossary for Japanese and Sanskrit names and terms.)

Amitābha (Skt; J: Amida): The Buddha of Infinite Light, whose forty-eight vows epitomize the bodhisattva spirit of boundless compassion. According to Shin Buddhists, anyone who calls upon Amitabha's name with deep faith will be reborn in the Western paradise, the Pure Land, where Amitabha is said to reside.

angō (J) (lit. "peaceful dwelling"): A practice period, usually three months in length, devoted to meditation, study, and communal work.

anuttara samyak sambodhi (Skt): Literally, supreme perfect enlightenment.

Avalokiteśvara (Skt; J: Kannon, Kanzeon): One of the principal bodhisattvas in the Zen Buddhist tradition, Avalokitesvara is the personification of great compassion and is usually represented in the female form.

Avatamsaka Sutra (Skt; Ch: *Hua-yen ching*; J: *Kegon kyo*) (lit. "garland sutra"): Said to be the teachings of Shakyamuni Buddha during the three weeks immediately following his great enlightenment, the *Avatamsaka Sutra* teaches the mutual interdependence and interpenetration of all phenomena and is the basic text of the Hua-yen school.

Blue Cliff Record (Ch: *Pi-yen lu*; J: *Hekigan roku*): A collection of one hundred koans compiled, with appreciatory verses, by Master Hsüeh-tou Ch'ung-hsien (J: Setcho Juken, 980–1052) and with commentaries by Master Yüan-wu K'o-ch'in (Engo Kokugon, 1063-1135). A text of fundamental importance for koan study in the Rinzai school, the *Blue Cliff Record* was also studied by Dogen Zenji, who brought back a handwritten copy when he returned to Japan from China.

bodhi-mandala (Skt): Refers to the place of enlightenment, which has no particular location but is seen everywhere by the penetrating eye of prajna wisdom.

bodhi-mind: The mind in which an aspiration to enlightenment has been awakened.

Bodhidharma (Skt; J: Daruma) (d. 532 AD): Known as the First Patriarch in China, Bodhidharma was the Indian master who brought Zen to China. According to tradition he sat in a cave doing zazen for nine years before transmitting the Dharma to Hui-k'o, the Second Patriarch (*Gateless Gate* Case, 41). Attributed to Bodhidharma is the famous four-line verse characterizing Zen:

> A special transmission outside the scriptures
> No dependence on words and letters.
> Seeing directly into the mind of man,
> Realizing true nature, becoming Buddha.

bodhisattva (Skt) (lit. "enlightenment being"): One who practices the Buddha way and compassionately foregoes final enlightenment for the sake of helping others become enlightened. The exemplar in Mahayana Buddhism.

Book of Equanimity (Ch: *Ts'ung-jung lu*; J: *Shoyo roku*): A collection of one hundred koans following the pattern of the *Blue Cliff Record*, compiled, with appreciatory verses, by Master T'ien-tung Hung-chih (Tendo Wanshi, 1091-1157). In 1223, Master Wan-sung Hsing-hsiu (Bansho Gyoshu, 1166–1246) added commentaries and capping phrases. Though not as famous as the *Blue Cliff Record*, the *Book of Equanimity* is widely used in the Soto school and is known as a work of great depth and subtlety.

bosatsukai (J) (lit. "a meeting of bodhisattvas"): Can be used to refer to any group of Zen Buddhists who meet together for practice.

Buddha (lit. "awakened one"): A term which variously indicates: the historical Buddha Shakyamuni; enlightened persons who have attained Buddhahood; the essential truth, the true nature of all beings. *See also* Buddha-nature.

Buddha- Dharma (J: buppo): The true realization of life; the Way to follow in order to attain that realization according to the teachings of Shakyamuni Buddha.

Buddha-nature: The intrinsic nature of all beings; true nature, true self.

Buddha Way (J: butsudo): Basically the same meaning as Buddha-Dharma, though with more of a sense of actually setting foot on the Path.

buji Zen (J) (lit. "no-matter" Zen): An excessively casual attitude toward Zen discipline and training, based on the rationalization that since we are all fundamentally buddhas, we need not bother with practice, morality or realization.

capping phrase (J: jakugo): A pithy expression which concisely summarizes or comments upon part or all of a koan. Zen students who work with koans are traditionally required to present capping phrases as further evidence of their understanding.

Chao-chou Ts'ung-shen (Ch; J: Joshu Jushin) (778-897): One of the greatest masters of the T'ang dynasty, the golden age of Zen, Chao-chou became a disciple of Master Nan-ch'üan at the age of eighteen and continued to practice zazen for over one hundred years. He appears frequently in koans and is especially famous for the koan "Chao-chou's Dog". *See also* muji.

compassion (Skt: karuna): This aspect of practice is emphasized in Mahayana Buddhism, including Zen, especially in the precepts and the vow to save all sentient beings. Compassion is the natural outgrowth of prajna wisdom and the two invariably go hand in hand.

Dharma (Skt): The teachings of the Buddha; Truth; Buddhist doctrine; universal Law.

Dharma combat (or Dharma dialogue): Lively interchange in which two Zen students, or student and teacher, test and sharpen their understanding.

Dharma hall: A room or building in a monastery in which the abbot gives his talks on the Dharma; also combined in most places with the Buddha hall, in which services are held.

Dharma name: The name given to someone when he or she receives the precepts (jukai), thus formally becoming a Buddhist.

Dharma successor: A person deemed worthy by a Zen master to carry on his teaching lineage and authorized to hold dokusan, verify enlightenment experiences, and in turn name Dharma successors.

Dharma transmission: Designation of a person as a Dharma successor. *See also* inka, *shobogenzo nehan myoshin*

Dharmakāya (Skt; J: hosshin): One aspect of the threefold body of Buddha; the absolute beyond all discrimination.

dharmas (Skt): Phenomena; elements or constituents of existence.

dhyāna (Skt): Similar in meaning to samadhi. In early Buddhism the term referred to various stages of concentrated awareness. Its Chinese and Japanese equivalents (Ch'an and Zen, respectively) have broader implications. *See also* Zen

Diamond Sutra (Skt: *Vajracchedika Sutra*; J: *Kongo kyo*): Highly regarded by the Zen sect, it sets forth the doctrines of sunyata and prajna (q.v.). The Sixth Patriarch attained enlightenment upon hearing a phrase from this sutra.

Dōgen Kigen Zenji (1200–1253): After training for nine years under the Rinzai teacher Myozen, Dogen Zenji made the difficult journey to China, where he studied with and became Dharma successor to T'ien-t'ung Ju-ching (Tendo Nyojo) in the Soto Zen lineage. Considered the founder of the Japanese Soto school, Dogen Zenji established Eiheiji, the principal Soto training monastery, and is best known for his collection of Dharma essays, *Shobogenzo* (q.v.).

dōjō (J): A training center.

dokusan (J): A one-to-one encounter between Zen student and Zen master in which the student's understanding is probed and stimulated and in which the student may consult the teacher on any matters arising directly out of practice.

eightfold path: The fourth noble truth, in which Shakyamuni Buddha indicated the Way to put an end to suffering. The eightfold path consists of: right views, right thought, right speech, right action, right livelihood, right effort, right mindfulness, and right samadhi.

Eiheiji: One of the two main temples of the Soto school of Zen, founded by Dogen Zenji in 1243. While the characters literally mean "temple of eternal peace", they are also a reference to the era when Buddhism was believed to have been first introduced to China.

emptiness (Skt: sunyata): The fundamental nature of all phenomena.

enlightenment: Realization of one's true nature.

five desires: Money or wealth (*zai*); material things, including sex (*shiki*); food (*jiki*); fame (*myo*); and sleep (*sui*).

four noble truths: One of the earliest and most fundamental teachings of the Buddha concerning the character of life and the Way of Buddhist practice. It states that: 1) life is suffering (*dukkha*); 2) suffering has a cause; 3) there is a way to put an end to the cause of suffering; 4) the way to put an end to the cause of suffering is the eight-fold path.

four vows: "Sentient beings are numberless; I vow to save them. Desires are inexhaustible; I vow to put an end to them. The Dharmas are boundless; I vow to master them. The Buddha-way is unsurpassable; I vow to attain it." Zen students chant these vows daily as an expression of their aspiration.

Fukanzazengi (J) (lit. "universal promotion of the principles of zazen"): A brief, seminal work on how and why to sit zazen, by Dogen Zenji.

fusatsu (J; Skt: uposatha): A ceremony, dating back to the time of the historical Buddha, held once or twice a month in Zen for the purpose of renewing the vows. Fusatsu involves open atonement for one's past evil karma and a recitation of the names of the Buddha, the Three Treasures, and the four vows, interspersed with much bowing.

gakki (J): Memorial service.

Genjōkōan (J) (lit: "realization of ultimate reality"): One of the key chapters of Dogen Zenji's *Shobogenzo* and a seminal essay in Japanese Soto Zen, it explores with great subtlety the relationship between practice and realization.

great death: The point in deep samadhi where all sense of self and other, one and many, falls away. Immediately following on this great death is great rebirth, or great enlightenment.

great rebirth: Great enlightenment.

Hakuin Ekaku Zenji (1686–1769): The patriarch of Japanese Rinzai Zen, through whom all present-day Rinzai masters have their lineage. He systematized koan study as we know it today.

hara (J): The area of the lower abdomen which is the physical center of gravity of the human body, and which becomes a center of awareness in zazen.

Heart Sutra (Skt: *Prajnaparamita hridaya sutra*; J: *Hannya haramita shingyō*): The essence of the prajna paramita literature expressed in one page. Chanted daily in Zen temples everywhere, its central teaching is "form is emptiness, emptiness is form".

Hinayāna (Skt; J: shojo) (lit. "small vehicle): Strictly speaking, a term used disparagingly by Mahayana Buddhists to refer to eighteen schools of Buddhism of which Theravada is the only one extant today. More generally it is used to indicate Buddhists whose practice is excessively concerned with their own enlightenment, causing them to disregard the practice and enlightenment of others. *See also* Mahayana

Hotei (Ch: Pu-tai): The big, fat, happy bodhisattva often depicted with a large sack on his back and regarded as an incarnation of Maitreya. He is the one returning to the market place with helping hands in the last of the ten oxherding pictures, an embodiment of the bodhisattva ideal of teaching the Dharma in the midst of suffering and defilement.

inka (J): The special seal of approval given to highly accomplished Dharma successors who have completed koan study and have attained the maturity to guide students in koan study as well as in the practice of zazen.

jōriki (J) (lit. "samadhi power"): The vital, stabilizing energy arising from strong zazen practice.

jūkai (J): Ceremony of receiving the precepts. A person receiving the precepts formally becomes a Buddhist and is given a Dharma name.

kalpa (Skt): An eon; an extremely long period of time.

Kannon: *See* Avalokitesvara

karma (Skt): The principle of causality, which holds that for every effect there is a cause and, in the human sphere, maintains that by our actions we determine the quality of our lives and influence the lives of others.

Keizan Jōkin Zenji (1268–1325): Fourth patriarch and co-founder, with his predecessor Dogen Zenji, of the Soto school in Japan, Keizan Zenji was largely responsible for the spread of Japanese Soto Zen and was particularly noted for his meticulous instructions and procedures governing virtually every aspect of monastic life.

kenshō (J) (lit. "seeing into one's nature"): An experience of enlightenment; also known as satori.

kinhin (J): Walking zazen, usually done for five to ten minutes between periods of sitting zazen.

kōan (J): A brief anecdote recording an exchange between master and student or a master's enlightenment experience. Koans are used in Zen to bring a student to realization and to help clarify his enlightenment.

kōan study: The intensive, non-intellectual study of koans in Zen meditation. Conventional, discursive thinking is by-passed, and a student is encouraged to give spontaneous, direct responses that express the heart of the matter in question. Koan study helps a student learn the structure of the Dharma and sharpens his prajna eye.

kyosaku (J) (lit. "waking stick"): A long stick, generally flattened at one end, the kyosaku is carried in the meditation hall by one or more monitors who periodically whack sitters on the shoulders to encourage them or to help them stay awake.

Lin-chi I-hsüan (J: Rinzai Gigen) (d. 866): One of the great masters of the T'ang dynasty in China and founder of the Lin-chi school of Zen. Famous for his beating and shouting, Lin-chi is a Dharma successor of Huang-po Hsi-yün (Obaku Kiun).

Lotus Sutra (or *Sutra of the Lotus of the Wonderful Law*) (Skt: *Saddharma pundarika sutra*; J: *Myōhōrenge kyō*): An elaborate presentation, in prose and verse, of the Buddha's teaching that there is fundamentally only one vehicle to liberation and that all beings are able to attain perfect enlightenment. The basic text of the Tendai and Nichiren sects.

makyō (J) (lit. "demons of the objective world"): Illusions, fantasies, hallucinations; more generally, any phenomena or experiences which distract one from practice or to which one becomes attached.

Mahāparinirvana Sutra: A Mahayana scripture said to be the sermon preached by the Buddha just before his death; not to be confused with the Hinayana *Mahaparinibbana Suttanta* of the Pali canon, which deals with the last days and death of Shakyamuni. *See also* parinirvana

Mahāyāna (Skt; J: daijo) (lit. "great vehicle"): Refers to the type of Buddhism found throughout Tibet, China, Korea, Japan, and Viet Nam. It emphasizes compassion and the bodhisattva ideal of fore-going final nirvana to remain in the realm of birth and death to help suffering sentient beings. *See also* Hinayana

mandala: A diagrammatic representation of the universe in terms of the qualities of various buddhas and bodhisattvas, usually in the form of a circle. Used as an object of meditation in Tantric Buddhism. More generally, the term mandala refers to the constellation of one's karmic relationships at any given point in time.

Manjuśri (Skt; J: Monju): The bodhisattva of wisdom, often depicted riding a lion and holding the sword of wisdom which cuts through delusion. Especially appreciated in the Zen sect, Manjusri Bodhis-attva is the principal figure on the zendo altar. *See also* Avalokitesvara, Samantabhadra

muji (J): The character *mu*, a negative particle which is used to point directly at reality and has no discursive content. The use of the word in this sense originated with Master Joshu Jushin (Ch: Chao-chou, 778–897) who, when asked by a monk, "Does a dog have Buddha-nature?" directly answered "Mu!" The incident is used as the first koan in the *Gateless Gate* and is often the first koan encountered by Zen students in their koan study. The term *muji* is often used as a synonym of *emptiness* (q.v.).

nirvana (Skt; J: nehan): A non-dualistic state beyond life and death.

ōryōki (J) (lit. "that which holds just enough"): Broadly speaking, the nested set of eating bowls given every monk and nun at ordination. Strictly speaking the term refers exclusively to the largest of these bowls. In early Buddhist tradition, this bowl was used to collect offerings when the monk or nun would go begging in the street. Nowadays, oryoki are also used by laypersons.

pāramitās (Skt) (lit. "gone to the other shore"): The six perfections practiced by the bodhisattva, culminating with prajna paramita ("perfection of wisdom"), which informs and fulfills the other five. The paramitas are a natural expression of the enlightened mind, the mind of meditation. The six paramitas are: giving (*dana*); precepts or morality (*sila*); patience (*kshanti*); effort or vigor (*virya*); meditation (*dhyana*); and wisdom (*prajna*). Four more are sometimes added: skillfulness in means (*upaya*); determination (*pranidhana*); strength (*bala*); and knowledge (*jnana*).

parinirvana (Skt) (lit. "complete nirvana"): Refers to the dissolution of the five skandhas at the death of an enlightened being and his or her passing into final nirvana. *See also* nirvana

Patriarch: Strictly speaking, the first thirty-four Dharma successors from Shakyamuni Buddha through the Sixth Chinese Patriarch, Huineng (J: Eno, 638–713). More generally, an honorific term used to describe any Zen master of outstanding attainment.

prajnā (Skt; J: hannya): Enlightened wisdom.

precepts (Skt: sila; J: kai): Teachings regarding personal conduct, which can be appreciated on a fairly literal level as ethical guidelines and more broadly as aspects or qualities of reality itself. At the time of jukai, the Zen practicer receives and promises to maintain the following precepts. The Three Treasures: be one with the Buddha; be one with the Dharma; be one with the Sangha. The three pure precepts: do not commit evil; do good; do good for others. The ten grave precepts: do not kill; do not steal; do not be greedy; do not tell a lie; do not be ignorant; do not talk about others' faults; do not elevate yourself by criticizing others; do not be stingy; do not get angry; do not speak ill of the Three Treasures.

rakusu (J): Made of five strips of cloth and thus the smallest of the Buddhist robes (*kesa*), the rakusu is the only kesa worn by both monks and laypersons and is suspended from the neck by a cloth halter.

renewal of the vows: *See* fusatsu

Rinzai Gigen: *See* Lin-chi I-hsüan

Rinzai school: The Zen lineage founded by Master Lin-chi I-hsüan (Rinzai Gigen, d. 866).

Rōshi (J) (lit. "old teacher"): An honorific term used to refer to a Zen master.

samādhi (Skt; J: zammai): A state of mind characterized by one-pointedness of attention; a non-dualistic state of awareness.

Samantabhadra (Skt; J: Fugen): One of the three principal bodisattvas in the Zen Buddhist tradition, Samantabhadra is associated with practice and active love. *See also* Avalokitesvara, Manjusri

samu (J): Working zazen, often physical labor.

Sangha (Skt): Originally the community of Buddhist monks and nuns, the term Sangha later came to include laypersons as well. In Zen, the term sangha also connotes the harmonious interrelationship of all beings, phenomena, and events.

sanzen (J) (lit. "penetration [in] Zen"): In the Rinzai tradition, sanzen is synonymous with dokusan. For Dogen Zenji, founder of the Soto school in Japan, however, sanzen more broadly signifies the proper practice of zazen.

satori: *See* kensho

sesshin (lit. "to collect or regulate the mind"): A Zen meditation retreat, usually lasting one to seven days.

Shakyamuni (Skt) (lit. "the sage of the Shakya clan"): The title used to refer to Siddhartha Gautama, the historical Buddha, after his enlightenment.

shihō (J): Dharma transmission. *See also* inka

shikan-taza (J) (lit. "just sitting"): Zazen itself, without supportive devices such as breath-counting or koan study. Characterized by intense, non-discursive awareness, shikan-taza is "zazen doing zazen for the sake of zazen".

Shōbōgenzō (J) (lit. "treasury of the true Dharma eye"): Masterwork of Dogen Zenji, founder of the Japanese Soto school of Zen, it comprises some ninety-five articles dealing with a wide variety of Buddhist topics and is generally considered to be one of the most subtle and profound works in Buddhist literature.

shōbōgenzō nehan myōshin (J) (lit. "treasury of the true Dharma eye, marvelous mind of nirvana"): This phrase, attributed to the Buddha upon his transmission of the Dharma to Mahakasyapa, expresses the essence of Dharma transmission in which the minds of master and disciple become one.

shōsan (J): A formal meeting in Zen monasteries and centers in which a teacher or senior student gives a short talk and then engages in question/answer dialogue with any who wish to challenge his understanding, ask a question, or make a comment. A kind of public dokusan.

Sixth Patriarch Hui-neng (J: Eno, 638–713): Traditionally said to be illiterate, Hui-neng was enlightened while still a layman upon hearing a recitation of the *Diamond Sutra*. He became a Dharma successor of the Fifth Patriarch Hung-jen, and all lines of Zen now extant descend from him. His teaching, as recorded in the *Platform Sutra*, stresses "sudden enlightenment" (as opposed to the "gradual enlightenment" of the Northern School of Ch'an) and the identity of meditation (*dhyana*) and wisdom (*prajna*). He was largely responsible for the widespread flourishing of Zen in the T'ang Dynasty.

skandhas (Skt) (lit. "heaps, aggregates"): In Buddhist psychology, the five modes of being which, taken collectively, give rise to the illusion of self. They are: form, sensation, conception, discrimination and awareness.

Sōjiji: One of the two main temples of the Soto school of Zen, founded in 1321 after a long history as a Shingon temple.

Sōtō school: The Zen lineage founded by Masters Tung-shan Liang-chieh (Tozan Ryokai, 807–869) and Ts'ao-shan Pen-chi (Sozan Hon-jaku, 840–901). The Japanese branch was founded by Masters Dogen Kigen (1200–1253) and Keizan Jokin (1268–1325).

śunyatā: *See* emptiness

sutra (Skt) (lit. "thread"): Buddhist scripture; a dialogue or sermon attributed to the Buddha.

tantō (J): The person in charge of the operations of a zendo.

Tathāgata (Skt; J: Nyorai): The name the Buddha used in referring to himself; literally means "thus-come" or "thus-gone", indicating the enlightened state.

teishō (J): A formal commentary by a Zen master on a koan or other Zen text. In its strictest sense, teisho should be non-dualistic and is thus distinguished from Dharma talk, which is an ordinary lecture on some Buddhist topic.

ten oxherding pictures: Of ancient origin, they represent a step-by-step guide to the bodhisattva path, beginning with the stage of searching for the ox, in which the desire to practice is awakened, and ending with the return to the marketplace, in which both enlightenment and unenlightenment are transcended and the bodhisattva remains, freely functioning in the world of delusion. Actually, one passes through this entire cycle in each moment of practice.

ten realms: The realms of buddhas, bodhisattvas, pratyeka-buddhas, sravaka-buddhas, heavenly beings, human beings, fighting spirits, animals, hungry ghosts, and hell-dwellers.

tenzō (J): Person in charge of the kitchen in a monastery or Zen center. Traditionally, the position of tenzo is considered to be one of the most challenging assignments.

Three Treasures (J: sambō): Buddha, Dharma, and Sangha.

three worlds: 1) The worlds of desire, form, and formlessness. 2) Past, present, and future.

tokudo (J): Ceremony of receiving the precepts. There are two kinds of tokudo: *zaike* tokudo, in which one formally becomes a lay Buddhist; and *shukke* tokudo, in which one becomes a monk or a nun.

Tung-shan Liang-chieh (Ch; J: Tōzan Ryokai, 807–869): Principal founder of the Chinese Soto school. Famous for setting forth the teaching of the five positions (J: goi) and for his poem *Pao-ching sanmei* (J: *Hokyo Zammai* [Most Excellent Mirror Samadhi]), Tung-shan was noted for his meticulous practice and expression of the Dharma.

vinaya (Skt): (lit. "discipline"): The Buddhist school which most strongly emphasizes monastic discipline as the basis of its practice; generally, the code of conduct upon which this discipline is based.

Wan-sung Hsing-hsiu (Ch; J: Banshō Gyōshū, 1166–1246): Chinese Soto Zen master who added commentaries and capping phrases to the 100 koans collected by Hung-chih Cheng-chüeh in the *Ts'ung-jung lu* (J: *Shoyo roku* [*Book of Equanimity*]).

wu-wei (lit. "unconditioned"): Non-action, i.e., activity in which there is no dichotomy between the one doing and what is done, and which thus is unconditioned by subject and object, time and space, activity and non-activity. Wu-wei indicates the heart of Zen practice in daily life.

Yün-men Wen-yen (Ch; J: Ummon Bun'en, 863 –949): Founder of the Yün-men (Ummon) school, later absorbed into the Lin-chi (Rinzai) school. Yün-men's clear and concise answers to students' questions appear often in the major koan collections.

zafu (J) (lit. "sitting cushion"): Round cushion used for zazen.

zazen (J) (lit. "sitting meditation"): The practice of Zen meditation.

zendō (J): A place set aside for the practice of zazen.

zenji (J) (lit. "Zen master"): An honorific term used to refer to a master of high rank or attainment.

Chinese-Japanese Name Glossary

Since Japanese readings of Chinese names are used in the first two volumes of the *On Zen Practice* trilogy, we offer this glossary, which lists Chinese names and their Japanese equivalents.

Chinese to Japanese

Chao-chou Ts'ung-shen: Jōshū Jūshin
Ch'ing-yüan Hsing-ssu: Seigen Gyōshi
Chü-shih: Gutei
Fa-yen Wen-i: Hōgen Bun'eki
Hsüan-sha Shih-pei: Gensha Shibi
Hsüeh-feng I-ts'un: Seppō Gison
Hsüeh-tou Ch'ung-hsien: Setchō Jūken
Huang-po Hsi-yün: Ōbaku Kiun
Hui-k'o: Eka (2nd Patriarch)
Hui-neng: Enō (6th Patriarch)
Hung-jen: Gunin (5th Patriarch)
Kuei-shan Ling-yu: Isan Reiyū
Kuo Ning-chih: Kaku Jōza
Lin-chi I-hsüan: Rinzai Gigen
Lo-han Kuei-ch'en: Rakan Keijin
Lu-tsu: Roso
Ma-tsu Tao-i: Baso Dōitsu
Mu-chou: Bokujū
Nan-ch'üan P'u-yüan: Nansen Fugan
Nan-yüeh Huai-jang: Nangaku Ejō
Pai-chang Huai-hai: Hyakujō Ekai
Seng-ts'an: Sōsan (3rd Patriarch)
Shen-hsiu: Jinshū
Shih-shuang Ch'u-yüan: Sekisō Soen
Shih-t'ou Hsi-ch'ien: Sekitō Kisen
Ta-hui Tsung-kao: Daie Sōkō
Tan-hsia T'ien-jan: Tanka Tennen
Tao-hsin: Dōshin (4th Patriarch)
Tao-wu Yüan-chih: Dōgo Enchi
Te-shan Hsüan-chien: Tokusan Senkan
T'ien-lung: Tenryū
T'ien-t'ung Hung-chih: Tendō Wanshi
T'ien-t'ung Ju-ching: Tendō Nyojō
Ts'ao-shan Pen-chi: Sōzan Honjaku
Tung-shan Liang-chieh: Tōzan Ryōkai
Wan-sung Hsing-hsiu: Banshō Gyōshū
Wu-men Hui-k'ai: Mumon Ekai
Yen-t'ou Chüan-huo: Gantō Zenkatsu
Yen-yang: Gonyo
Yüan: En (Ummon's attendant)
Yüan-wu K'o-ch'in: Engo Kokugon
Yün-chü Tao-ying: Ungo Dōyō
Yün-men Wen-yen: Ummon Bun'en
Yün-yen T'an-sheng: Ungan Donjo

Japanese to Chinese

Banshō Gyōshū: Wan-sung Hsing-hsiu
Baso Dōitsu: Ma-tsu Tao-i
Bokujū: Mu-chou
Daie Sōkō: Ta-hui Tsung-kao
Dōgo Enchi: Tao-wu Yüan-chih
Dōshin: Tao-hsin (4th Patriarch)
Eka: Hui-k'o (2nd Patriarch)
En: Yüan (Ummon's attendant)
Engo Kokugon: Yüan-wu K'o-ch'in
Eno: Hui-neng (6th Patriarch)
Gantō Zenkatsu: Yen-t'ou Chüan-huo
Gensha Shibi: Hsüan-sha Shih-pei
Gonyo: Yen-yang
Gunin: Hung-jen (5th Patriarch)
Gutei: Chü-shih
Hōgen Bun'eki: Fa-yen Wen-i
Hyakujō Ekai: Pai-chang Huai-hai
Isan Reiyū: Kuei-shan Ling-yu
Jinshū: Shen-hsiu
Jōshū Jūshin: Chao-chou Ts'ung-shen
Kaku Jōza: Kuo Ning-chih
Mumon Ekai: Wu-men Hui-k'ai
Nangaku Ejō: Nan-yüeh Huai-jang
Nansen Fugan: Nan-ch'üan P'u-yüan
Ōbaku Kiun: Huang-po Hsi-yün
Rakan Keijin: Lo-han Kuei-ch'en
Rinzai Gigen: Lin-chi I-hsüan
Roso: Lu-tsu
Seigen Gyōshi: Ch'ing-yüan Hsing-ssu
Sekisō Soen: Shih-shuang Ch'u-yüan
Sekitō Kisen: Shih-t'ou Hsi-ch'ien
Seppō Gison: Hsüeh-feng I-ts'un
Setchō Jūken: Hsüeh-tou Ch'ung-hsien
Sōsan: Seng-ts'an (3rd Patriarch)
Sōzan Honjaku: Ts'ao-shan Pen-chi
Tanka Tennen: Tan-hsia T'ien-jan
Tendō Wanshi: T'ien-t'ung Hung-chih
Tendō Nyojō: T'ien-t'ung Ju-ching
Tenryū: T'ien-lung
Tokusan Senkan: Te-shan Hsüan-chien
Tōzan Ryōkai: Tung-shan Liang-chieh
Ummon Bun'en: Yün-men Wen-yen
Ungan Donjō: Yün-yen T'an-sheng
Ungo Dōyō: Yün-chü Tao-ying

Index

Cumulative Index

(for *On Zen Practice I*, *On Zen Practice II*, and *The Hazy Moon of Enlightenment* (*On Zen Practice III*))

103–4; III: 49–55, 160n
chanting, I: 38
Chao-chou Ts'ung-shen (Joshu
Jushin), I: 107; II: 81–89, 100–4; III:
54, 121
Ch'ing-yüan Wei-hsin (Seigen Ishin),
III: 153
Chu-chih (Gutei), II: 43
classless treasury of the true Dharma
eye, marvelous mind of nirvana.
See shobogenzo nehan myoshin
compassion, I: 11, 60; III: 10, 15, 47,
110, 157
conceit, III: 85
concentration. See samadhi
consciousness, eight kinds of, II: 76;
III: 91, 146
consistency, III: 112–13
continuous practice, spiral of, III: 10,
62, 78, 115

Daito Kokushi, III: 101
Daitsu Chisho Buddha. See
Mahabhijna Jnanabhibu Buddha
delusion, III: 2, 27, 57–64, 85
Denko roku. See Transmission of the Light
desire(s), III: 10, 69–70, 83–87
determination, III: 114
Dharma, I: 5, 24, 41, 60, 64, 87–88,
100–1, 119; II: 1, 13–15, 59, 68, 78,
118
different aspects of, III: 142
as enlightened Way taught by
Buddha, III: 8, 18, 20, 71–73, 92,
120–26, 142–43 (see also Buddha-
Dharma)
stinking of, III: 17
three periods of, III: 8
as one of the Three Treasures, III:
121–26, 155
transmission of, II: 98; III: 7, 110
Dharma-attachment, III: 37, 44, 46
Dharma-vehicle, II: 13, 20
Dharmakaya, I: 60, 64–65, 114; III: 37,
44–45, 51, 55

Diamond Sutra, III: 50–51, 130
differences, III: 45, 49–50, 112, 142
Dogen Zenji, I: 1, 3, 7–9, 18, 29–33,
41, 63, 65, 87, 91, 96; III: 9, 10, 55,
62–63, 111, 115
as the author of "The Eight
Awarenesses", III: 77–78
on bowing, II: 59
Eiheikoroku, I: 1; II: ix
on enlightenment, II: 7–12, 67, 73,
78, 79
on faith, II: 69, 79
Fukanzazengi, I: 96, 120; II: 8, 13–
52, 69; III: 5
Genjokoan, III: 55, 141
and great doubt, III: 113
on the precept of not killing, II:
96, 102
Shobogenzo, II: 17, 18; III: 74, 77
on whole-hearted practice, II: 2,
73, 79
dokusan, I: 46–47, 120; II: 80, 106
doubt, III: 31, 85, 113
dualism, III: 8, 15, 43, 51, 102, 104,
105. See also differences
dullness & distraction, in zazen, II: 15

effort, I: 18, 26–31; III: 71, 78, 109–13
meticulous, defined, III: 111
ego, II: 27
eight awarenesses (of the enlightened
person), III: 69–80, 85–86, 120
"Eight Awarenesses of the
Enlightened Person" (Dogen
Zenji), I: 26–28; III: 74, 77
translation of, III: 69–74
eightfold path, III: 77–78, 120
Eiheiji, III: 77
Eiheikoroku, (Dogen Zenji) selection
from, I: 1; II: ix
Emperor Wu, I: 74
emptiness (sunyata), I: 25, 60, 122; III:
30, 43–44, 51, 142
of subject and object, III: 57–58
Enin Bussho, II: 1

188   Cumulative Index

Ta-hui Tsung-kao (Daie Soko), III: 137
Takuju, I: 58–59
tanden-kikai, II: 73
Tan-hsia Ti'en-jan (Tanka Tennen), II: 104
Tao-wu Yüan-chih (Dogo Enchi), I: 116
Tathagata, III: 8, 57, 59, 121
Te-shan Hsüan-chien (Tokusan Senkan), I: 105, 117; III: 17
teisho, I: 52, 58, 122
ten oxherding pictures, II: 24, 75; III: 10
Tendai Buddhism. See T'ien-t'ai Buddhism
tenzo, I: 39
three poisons, III: 23, 140. See also anger; greed; ignorance
Three Treasures, I: 5; II: 58–61, 90, 93, 96, 99, 117; III: 79, 120–26
three realms. See three worlds
three worlds (three realms), III: 130, 133–34
T'ien-lung (Tenryu), II: 45
T'ien-t'ai (Tendai) Buddhism, II: 78; III: 159n
T'ien-t'ung Hung-chih (Tendo Wanshi), I: 103; III: 52–53, 137, 159n
Toku joza, I: 114
tokudo. See also jukai
   shukke, II: 91, 107
   zaike, II: 91, 108
Torei Zenji, III: 110
tranquility (serenity), III: 70, 79, 99–104
transmission, II: 98
Transmission of the Light, III: 4
true nature. See Buddha-nature
true self. See Buddha-nature
Ts'an t'ung ch'i (Sandokai), III: 43
Ts'ao-shan Pen-chi (Sozan Honjaku), I: 114
Tung-shan Liang-chieh (Tozan Ryokai), I: 66, 69, 109; III: 10, 52, 101–2

upaya. See expedient means

views, wrong, III: 85
Vimalakirti, I: 108; III: 11
Vimalakirti Nirdesa Sutra, I: 108; III: 11
void. See emptiness
vows. See four vows

Wan-sung Hsing-hsiu (Bansho Gyoshu), I: 103; III: 41, 49–55, 160n
Watanabe Genshu Zenji, III: 5
wisdom (prajna), I: 11, 20, 30, 60, 73, 89, 99, 120; II: 76–78, 87; III: 84, 131
   Buddha's, III: 5
   and compassion, III: 10, 157
   cultivating, III: 72, 139–48
   as one of the eight awarenesses, III: 77
   of equality, III: 141, 146
worldly involvement, III: 70, 103
Wu-men Hui-k'ai (Mumon Ekai), I: 68, 85; II: 85, 87, 102; III: 9
wu-wei. See non-doing

Yakushi Nyorai, II: 47
Yasutani Roshi, Hakuun, I: 7, 8, 59, 64, 65, 88; II: 11, 24, 40, 41, 45, 47; III: 134
Yen-t'ou Chüan-huo (Ganto Zenkatsu), I: 110–11, 117; III: 16, 152
Yen-yang (Gonyo), III: 54, 121
Yüan-wu K'o-ch'in (Engo Kokugon), II: 105
yuishiki. See mind-only
Yün-chü Tao-ying (Ungo Doyo), III: 101–2
Yün-men Wen-yen (Ummon Bun'en), III: 16, 37–55, 58, 60, 134, 159n
Yün-men (Ummon) school, III: 41
"Yün-men's Two Sicknesses", III: 37–63 passim, 160n
Yün-yen T'an-sheng (Ungan Donjo), I: 109, 116
zazen, I: 4, 8, 15, 18, 19, 25, 32, 38, 44, 45, 91–92, 94, 96, 97, 122; II: 11, 14, 15, 18, 78; III: 7, 60, 64, 96, 111

defined, III: 100. *See also* breathing
in zazen; posture in zazen;
shikan-taza

Zen, III: 13–20
   beat, III: 125
   buji, III: 15
   delusion-and-realization, III: 15–
   16, 18
   gradual-enlightenment, III: 15–16
   proximate, III: 15, 18
   quiet meditative, III: 14, 18
   self-nature, III: 17–18
   sudden-enlightenment, III: 15, 17

ABOUT THE AUTHORS

Hakuyū Taizan Maezumi—One of the most accessible and effective Zen masters in America today, Taizan Maezumi Roshi devotes all of his time and energy to his various functions as director and spiritual mentor of the Zen Center of Los Angeles and editor of the Zen Writings series.

Born in his father's temple in 1931, Maezumi Roshi was ordained a Soto Zen monk at the age of eleven, and after receiving degrees in Oriental literature and philosophy from Komazawa University, studied at Sojiji, one of the two main Soto monasteries in Japan. In 1956 he came to the United States, studying English at Pasadena City College and at San Francisco State. Ten years later he founded the Zen Center of Los Angeles and began receiving students.

Maezumi Roshi has completed koan study and received *inka* (approval as a teacher) from both Koryu Osaka Roshi and Hakuun Yasutani Roshi, thus becoming Dharma successor to two major lines of Rinzai Zen. Dharma successor also to his father, Hakujun Kuroda Roshi, Maezumi Roshi is unique in having received Dharma transmission within both the Soto and Rinzai traditions.

Bernard Tetsugen Glassman—At the end of the summer of 1977, Bernard Tetsugen Glassman, Sensei, Assistant Director of the Zen Center of Los Angeles and co-editor of the Zen Writings series, received Dharma transmission from Taizan Maezumi Roshi, thus becoming Maezumi Roshi's first Dharma successor. Gen Sensei has completed koan study in the Harada Roshi/Yasutani Roshi line, and now assists Maezumi Roshi in guiding students in their practice

Born in Brooklyn, N.Y., in 1939, Gen Sensei received a doctorate in mathematics from UCLA and worked as an administrator and engineer in the aerospace industry for fifteen years. He began practicing with Maezumi Roshi in 1968, was ordained a monk two years later, and in 1973 was made head monk of the Zen Center. He and his wife Helen live at the Center with their two children.

Hakuun Ryōko Yasutani (1885–1973)—Ordained at the age of eleven, Yasutani Roshi studied as a young monk with several well-known masters. In 1925, after sixteen years as a school-teacher in Tokyo, he became the disciple of Daiun Sogaku Harada Roshi, from whom he received *inka* (approval as a teacher) in 1943. Between 1962 and 1969, Yasutani Roshi made frequent visits to the United States and in 1970, less than three years before his death at the age of eighty-eight, he named Hakuyu Taizan Maezumi, head priest at the Zen Center of Los Angeles, as a Dharma successor. Like his teacher Harada Roshi, Hakuun Yasutani Roshi borrowed freely from Soto and Rinzai traditions, recommending both koan study and shikan-taza to his students.

Daiun Sōgaku Harada (1870–1961)—Daiun Harada Roshi was a Zen master of rare breadth and accomplishment in twentieth-century Japan. Ordained a Soto monk at the age of seven, he studied as a young man at the Rinzai monastery of Shogenji. At the age of forty, after nearly ten years of scholastic study at Komazawa University, he became the personal attendant of Dokutan Roshi, abbot of Nanzenji and one of the best Zen masters of the day. After completing koan study with Dokutan Roshi and becoming his Dharma successor, Harada Roshi became abbot of Hosshinji and during the next forty years, until his death in 1961, made that monastery famous as a rigorous Zen training center, known for its harsh climate, its strict discipline and its abbot's keen Zen eye.

The paulownia leaves-and-flowers design is the trademark of Center Publications, publishers of fine books on Zen, Buddhism, and the arts. Director: John Daido Loori. Editor: Stephan Ikko Bodian. Photography: John Daido Loori. Production: Brenda Chiko Beck, Larry Watson. Typeset in Palatino by Chapman's Phototypesetting, Fullerton, CA. Printed & bound by Edwards Brothers, Ann Arbor, Michigan.